Flipping Houses Exposed

34 Weeks in The Life of a
Successful House Flipper

Danny Johnson
FlippingJunkie.com

*This book is dedicated to my family because they put up with my craziness and constant tapping away at my computer.
My family is my life and I wouldn't be where I am without them.
And that's a fact.*

Table of Contents

Preface

_____

Originally written in 2013.

Why expose my house flipping business so that everyone can see what my wife and I have been doing to successfully flip houses for over 10 years?

That's a question I've often asked myself when I consider how much I'm giving away to my competition. We are still flipping houses and the competition has become fierce again. Showing all my cards can't be smart, can it?

The reason behind sharing everything we did in our business for 34 weeks was originally done on my blog, FlippingJunkie.com. I needed to get my butt back in gear after taking it easy for a while. After reading real estate investing forums and coming across several threads where people talked about getting started and asked everyone to hold them accountable, I figured that would be a good way to get going again. I could share what I was doing with everyone so that they could follow along and learn about the _real_ world of house flipping.

This turned into an incredible series of posts that went further to help other people understand how house flipping works and what is really involved than any other source out there. I wanted to create this book to help those of you interested in learning how to flip houses do so by watching over my shoulder as I showed everything I was doing week to week.

This business has allowed a lot of people to create a life they've always wanted, to be their own boss, to call the shots, to be able to vacation when, where, and for as long as they want. It's a creative outlet that allows you to really enjoy life and escape the rat race and the trading of hours for dollars.

But, it's not a get-rich-quick, working 4 hours a week in your underwear type of business. It takes hard work and dedication. Despite that, I have fun running my flipping business and it is well worth the work. This book will show you what I mean.

The Story

My wife and I have been investing in real estate for over 10 years in San Antonio, TX. For the last several years, we've typically bought and sold between 25 and 30 houses a year. Our exit strategy is usually to fix and flip retail, but we also wholesale houses and sell some with owner financing for long-term cash flow.

Here's what happened and what I am doing about it:

Last summer, my family took a vacation to the west coast. We went from San Diego to Seattle over three weeks, stopping in the major cities and San Simeon. What a beautiful place!

Seeing Howard Hughes' "Spruce Goose" was on my list of things I wanted to do and so we visited the Air and Space Museum in McMinnville, OR. Being there really rekindled my desire to learn how to fly — I've wanted to learn for the last several years.

So, as soon as we got back, I started researching flying schools and taking flights with different instructors. For several months, all I was doing was thinking about flying. Investing took a back seat and I was playing "semi-retired."

I ended up passing my check ride in November and immediately realized (now that my brain was starting to allow other thoughts in) that we had quite an inventory of houses waiting to be rehabbed. (I would never wish rehabbing 6 houses at one time on anybody!) We also had some that were already finished that were just sitting on the market.

Over the new year, the market got really slow and I was hesitant to pick up any more, especially because I was so worn out from dealing with contractors and rehabbing issues, which is the hardest part of this business in my opinion.

Fast forward to today. The houses are all finished and on the market and we are getting them under contract. I now need to fill my deal pipeline again. I feel like I am starting over because what you experience today is usually a result of what you did over the last 3-6 months—and for me, that was very little outside of flying.

I have decided to share, with whoever is interested, the process of finding and generating leads, closing deals, rehabbing houses, and re-selling them. I am going to show how I market myself and document the leads that come in, the analysis I do, the purchases I make, and the entire rehabbing and selling process.

This is a great opportunity for me to track my results and for you to see how a successful real estate investing business operates.

In the following chapters, you'll find:

- My lead generation process and analysis
- The offers I make and how I decide on the offer amount
- Houses I've put under contract and what I do with them
- The rehab and re-sale process
- The final flip analysis with detailed deal numbers

Follow along week by week, and you'll see how I turned 505 leads into 11 deals that made me nearly $250,000 and a home we now call ours.

How to use this book

In the chapters to come, I'll lay out exactly what I did each week of the process, including the leads I got, my analysis of them, progress on current deals, and the results of those deals.

Originally, this book was written as a series of blog posts with details of each and every lead I analyzed. To make it more appropriate for a book, I've changed it up a bit and included the lead details on only the most interesting leads and situations. I've also included a primer for anyone who doesn't know how house flipping works in the Introduction. Here, you'll learn about what I do to generate leads and how I negotiate and manage all the deals I come across. I would recommend you start here, even if you are familiar with flipping.

In the main body of the book, you'll find weekly reports on my leads and progress, where I tell you what I did that week and which leads I followed.

At the end of the book, you'll find the Flipped Houses section where I detail each deal I made, what went into that deal, how I rehabbed or wholesaled the property and the results. I also link to before and after photos for your interest.

Now that you know the plan and how it should work, let's get into it.

Introduction

Over the course of this book — my 34-week process — I'll show you exactly what I've done each week to find, buy and flip houses. But before we get into that, I want to tell you more about my overall process and what I do on a regular basis.

I'm a full-time real estate investor and spend most of my days on the phone or computer checking into leads and making deals. I also visit a lot of houses, deal with contractors, manage house rehabs, and pass leads on to other investors.

The entire flipping process is not overly complicated, but some explanation is warranted. I use a mix of conventional and unconventional tactics to make deals and figure out if a deal is worth it for me. To start off this book, let's get into how I generate leads.

Generating leads

The biggest job of any real estate investor is to find properties that are available and gain an edge over competitors by getting there first and offering a great deal for (hopefully!) both sides. I use several different techniques for generating these leads, including paid advertising, searching listings, connecting with real estate agents, and my buying website. These are all methods you can use yourself to get people on the phone, talking to you about their house.

Buying website

My buying website, DannyBuysHouses.com, pulls in a good amount of leads every month. It's a straightforward site where anyone who's looking for an offer can submit their contact information and address to get an offer from me. I usually will then contact each person to find out more about their house and their situation.

The website also features testimonials from past owners, a bit of information about me, and an FAQ section. It is well worth the small investment and I was able to build it myself (I have a background in software development). I usually include my website in my other forms of marketing.

I actually offer websites for real estate investors that include all of the knowledge I've learned over nearly a decade of using one to get most of my leads. You can find out more and get one for yourself at http://leadpropeller.com/flippinghousesexposed

Bandit signs

In my opinion, bandit signs kick butt! These are signs I have other people put up around town that just have my phone number and basic information:

On about a monthly or bi-monthly basis, I have my contractor put out about 40 bandit signs in a certain target area of mine. I target houses that retail between $85,000 and $150,000, as that is what the majority of qualifying people in San Antonio are buying.

I pay my guy $2 per sign to put them out at busy intersections along the main thoroughfares. If you are just starting out, putting them out yourself the first couple of times will give you a good idea of where the best locations to place them are, and will quickly show you why it is worth it to pay someone else to do it for you. I use 24x18 horizontal corrugated plastic signs nailed to posts.

I recommend you check for local restrictions regarding these signs as they are illegal in many cities—I've been called by the city a few times for having too many up or for leaving them up too long.

Overall, I find these signs one of the best ways to generate lots of leads. There are some weeks where they don't generate as many, but results over the long run are positive. Usually, people will call as soon as they see them, so be sure you've got your phone with you and you're able to answer when they call. Getting in early or being one of the first calls they make can be a huge advantage over your competitors.

Drive for Dollars

Driving for dollars is basically driving through neighborhoods looking for vacant, distressed houses. I usually go with my wife every month or so — sometimes less frequently if I'm busy. What we do is choose a target neighborhood that is prime for rehabbing — one where we've had good deals in the past--usually not too run down, but not upscale either.

When we find a potential house, we write down the address and leave a door hanger or flyer. Sometimes, we also stop and talk to people working on other rehab jobs in the area and see what kind of materials they are using.

After driving around and collecting addresses, I usually look up who the owners are and their mailing addresses through the county appraisal district's website and then send a handwritten letter (I usually hire someone for this part). If I don't hear back, I might send a few more letters.

I find driving for dollars does turn up good leads and the actual driving is relaxing and can be fun, especially as I go with my wife. It can be a bit of work, but I always track my leads, the letters I send, and the results I get.

I've put together a primer on driving for dollars that contains lessons learned from years of doing this. It's kind of a 'best practices' article that you can find at http://flippingjunkie.com/how-to-drive-for-dollars-a-primer/

$20 Marketing Cards

The $20 marketing cards actually look like folded $20 bills. If that doesn't catch someone's eye, I don't know what will — you can have lots of fun with them! These are cards you leave all over the place that have your marketing message on them.

Here's what mine looks like:

I got these from DollarCardMarketing.com. You should seriously consider getting them too!

Realtors, MLS, REO

We receive leads from Realtors all the time. The key is to build relationships with Realtors that list bank-owned properties. When banks foreclose and take houses back, they own them. They're banks and not real estate investors, so they typically want to sell these houses quickly to recover the money they paid out for the loan and each bank tends to work with a single agent in a city to sell these properties. These are the agents you need to become fast friends with.

Here are my best tips for becoming an REO agent's best friend:

1. Have funds ready to close fast. You will need to close the deal quickly and without hassle — cash is king. If you don't have the funds yourself, work on finding private lenders amongst your family and friends. If your family and friends are all broke, get pre-approved through some local hard money lenders. You should be able to find a reputable lender lending at about 12-14% interest with 1 point.

2. Don't ask the agents questions about the house. You've got to be a professional real estate investor that knows what he/she is doing. When you look at these houses, you will have questions, just don't waste the agent's time with questions like, "How old is the roof?" If you don't know what's important from a house flipper's perspective, find a local real estate investor that does lots of deals and pay them to show you.

3. Move fast. If they tell you about a house that is going on the market or that is already on the market, get your butt over there and look at it. Make an offer no matter what. You may not want the piece of junk, so make an offer that would be a no-brainer for you (i.e., you'd be able to sell it to another investor for more because you got it so cheap).

4. Call them regularly, but not every day. You want to be top-of-mind so that when they have a hot deal come across their desk, they are thinking of you. So stay in contact with them — use your best judgment to figure how often this should be as it varies with agents and how often they get these listings.

5. Meet with them. Don't do like the hundreds of lazy investors and just send them an email or call them once or twice. Invite them to lunch at their favorite restaurant and find out what they're interested in besides real estate. If they're local sports fans, get them tickets to a game. Set yourself apart from the herd of other investors that expect something for nothing.

You can find my interview with a top REO agent in San Antonio here: http://flippingjunkie.com/interview-with-a-top-reo-agent/

Referrals

We receive referral leads from time to time as well. Usually, these are awesome because they show that our service was so outstanding that a seller felt it necessary to tell someone else about us. Plus, it doesn't require any marketing dollars.

This is why it's so very important to treat each transaction as if it's your first. Go out of your way to make sure the seller is informed each step of the way as to what is happening. Make sure they don't have any unanswered questions.

You might think this is obvious, but when you've been in the business any length of time and have done quite a few deals, you'll find that buying a house becomes no big deal. It's hard to remember that, to the seller, it could be a *very* big deal. They may have grown up in the house and have lots of memories. Always remember that.

Wholesale

Basically, a wholesaler is a person or company that buys and sells properties for cheap on a quick turnaround. There are wholesalers in every market that become professionals at finding deals just to sell them to rehabbers and landlords.

Do you know who they are? You need to. They are spending thousands of dollars and countless hours turning over rocks looking for deals. You can buy them without all the effort of having to find them.

True, many of the deals you see blasted out by email are far from deals you or I would be interested in…but those aren't the only wholesale deals being sold. Many wholesalers have a short list of VIP buyers that buy most of their deals. Who do you think gets a call when they get a deal signed up and need to move it? The buyers who have proven themselves and bought other properties from them. You have to become one of these VIP buyers, so do the same things I mentioned for REO agents to become best friends with the top wholesalers in your market.

Yellow Pages

I've had a dollar-bill-sized ad in the yellow pages for the past four years. This form of marketing isn't the cheapest, but it does pay for itself. Every year, I question whether to keep it because of the near $1,000/month price tag, but after looking at my results, it is always a no-brainer to keep it.

Maybe it's a little over the top, but it sure does grab your attention. I decided to set myself apart from all of the other 'we buy houses' ads in the phone book.

FSBO

For sale by owner. This speaks for itself: people selling the house themselves. They're often in the paper, but more often online now: places like the newspaper classifieds and Craigslist. Usually, you'll find them in the neighborhoods where investors are fixing up houses.

To make this an effective route for generating leads, you need to drive neighborhoods all the time and call every single FSBO — you never know who is motivated to sell fast. Don't make the assumption that they are selling FSBO to save a buck and get top dollar; most FSBO sellers are doing that, but how many does it take that are just plain motivated to make you tens of thousands of dollars? Keep that in mind. Just one good deal will make weeks of calling FSBO well, well worth it.

Probate

Houses in probate are ones where the owner has passed away and the county is taking stock of their assets before completing the inheritance process. Probates are always public record, so I hire someone to go down to the county courthouse and go through probate records.

I have them look for probate files where the deceased had real property and if property was owned, I get the executor of the estate's name and address so that I can send them a letter.

I get mixed responses from these letters. There are some people who believe this is insensitive, but others who are happy to not have to look for someone to buy the house. Overall, the money I spend on this and the effort put in tends to be worthwhile at the end of the year.

Absentee owners

For absentee owners, what I typically do is get a list from a title company or listsource.com of properties and then send out postcards to the property owners letting them know I'm interested in their house and that I buy houses with cash.

Typically, I specify to only include absentee owners with 3 bedrooms or more, single-family homes and with 30% or more equity with a property value below $150,000. With these specifications, I can usually narrow down a list from 33,000 properties to several thousand highly targeted ones.

This year, right after I did the mailing, I had one woman who called telling me I was trying to steal houses in the neighborhood after they had finally resolved a long-lasting flooding problem. Of course, I had no idea the neighborhood had a flooding problem, but that didn't stop her.

You will get calls from people like this and you must do your best to be polite. You never know, one of these callers may call you in the future to sell a property. It surely adds a little excitement — I never got calls like that when I was working as a software developer!

Questions to Ask Sellers When They Call

Once you hear from a lead, you'll want to get on the phone with them as soon as possible. Some will contact you that way to start out, but others, like ones who find you online, will require you to call them. Either way, when you speak with a seller, you need to ask the right questions to be able to determine whether you should spend more time working on the lead. These are the questions I ask:

- What is the address of the house?
- How many bedrooms and bathrooms does the house have and is there a garage?
- Does the house need any repairs?
- Why are you selling the house?
- How much is owed?
- What are you looking to get for the house?
- Do you know what similar houses are selling for in the area?
- Is there anything that you do not like about the house?
- If they bought the house recently, how much did they put down? (If not much, a deal is probably not doable.)
- How fast do you need to have it closed?
- If I were to pay cash and close quickly, what is the least you would be willing to take? (You'll be amazed at how much below their asking price this will be.)
- How did you find out about me? (You want to keep track of the marketing that is pulling best.)

The questions aren't always in this exact order and are intended to be asked in the normal flow of conversation. You just need to direct the conversation so as to have these questions answered without seeming to be in a hurry and ignoring what they are telling you. They want to know you are really listening to them. Expand on their motivation to sell by asking open-ended questions. Over time, you will develop your own style.

Calculating repairs

When you're in the house flipping game, it would be impossible to go visit all the leads you get before making an offer. I usually speak with them on the phone first and find out what they are willing to take. If a deal seems possible, I will usually go see the house to ensure the repairs aren't going to be more than anticipated.

When I go into a house, I can come up with a cost estimate in about 10 minutes using Ron Legrand's method. Some people call it crazy, but I know it works. Basically, you will never get the estimate exactly right. No matter how detailed you get, you will never be exactly right with the actual costs. So, go in and determine whether the job will cost $5k (kind of hard these days), $10k, $15k, $20k, etc. Multiples of $5k. When the estimate comes to roughly $17k, round it to $20k.

This is usually hard for new investors to do. To help get an idea, the best way is to take an experienced investor with you. If you don't know any that will go with you, take a contractor. Just be careful to not overdo it. You are not going to live in the house. Be mindful of the price range and don't go putting granite in a house that will retail for $60,000 (or $125,000 for that matter). Spend lots of time at Home Depot or Lowe's getting an idea of what materials cost.

Of course, you will make mistakes, but don't worry so much. You should be buying the house cheap enough that you should never have to worry about burning up all of your profits. You won't likely lose money, but you might make less than you figured.

Speaking of mistakes, I remember one argument I had with a contractor when I first started. I actually argued with him over the cost of quarter-round trim. He was trying to tell me they were $60 for the amount needed and I told him that I just saw them at Home Depot for $0.75 for 8' or 10' lengths and that did not add up to $60. We argued for about five minutes and I got my way. Well...I was walking through Home Depot a couple days later and had to take a look. I was shocked to find out that I was looking at the cost per foot! An apology was made immediately. How embarrassing.

Deciding to make an offer

What do I consider when deciding to make an offer? Almost nothing. For sure, if I go to see a house, I'm going to make an offer. Maybe I don't want the piece of turd — in that case, I'll make a super low-ball offer that I know is low enough to allow me to sell it quickly to another investor that likes turds.

Even if the seller doesn't seem motivated in the least, I will still make an offer. Why not? What have you got to lose? You've already spent time on the deal, so make an offer no matter what. Even in cases where your maximum allowable offer ends up being lower than what they owe on the house, make an offer anyway! We've had sellers come to the table with tens of thousands of dollars just to be done with the house. This happens more often than you think.

Now, if I talk to a seller on the phone and they are asking more than the house is worth completely fixed up and owe nearly the same, I won't even go to see it. It's a waste of time. Don't waste their time and don't waste yours. Tell them that you're sorry but you provide a fast and simple way to sell their house and you need to buy at below market value.

So, how do I decide what to offer? Usually, I use this simple formula:

70% of after repaired value (ARV) - repairs
= maximum allowable offer (MAO)

You take the amount the house will be worth after it's fixed up and multiply that by 70%. The 30% will be your profit and cover holding and closing costs. You then subtract your repairs estimate from the 70% of ARV and that gives you the MAO. Do not pay more than MAO! There are times where you will be tempted to, but don't.

Note: You'll notice throughout this book that I routinely used 65% and even 60% of ARV when calculating offers. This is because the market was still really soft after the 2008 downturn.

Notice how the formula doesn't account for how much is owed by the seller or their asking price? That's on purpose. That doesn't matter. What matters is what you need to buy it for. That might sound obvious, but visit with just a couple of sellers and watch how fast you start weighing how much they want for the house when determining how much you're going to offer. It's human nature to want to please other people. You can please people all day long if you want, but that needs to be separate from your business — start a charity for that.

If I'm not too worried about competition (they're not telling me they are speaking to other investors), I'll start somewhere around $5k to $10k below my maximum allowable offer. If they counter or just say that's not enough, I'll come up about $2,000. If they counter again, I'll come up $1,000. If they counter again, I'll come up $500. You see what's happening here? My increases are getting smaller. They will see that and know they won't get any more.

Other negotiating tips that have done well for us over the years:

1. Be confident in your offer. Do not beat around the bush and explain your offer for 10 minutes. Let them know what it is and act as though it's an incredible deal for them to be able to sell fast.

2. Be comfortable with long silences. Make your offer and shut up. Even if it takes a full minute for them to say something, let them say something before saying anything else. This can be hard to do at first, but it's an incredible skill to have. Nobody likes uncomfortable silences.

3. Negotiate items from the house as part of the deal and then remove them if you have to go back and forth on price. Do they have a motorcycle in the garage? Write the offer up to include it. If you don't agree on price, tell them you can remove it from the offer. In this example, you wouldn't want to do this if they mention how much they love the motorcycle; they might turn down your offer just because you included it in there.

Bird-dogging

In addition to actually buying and selling houses, I make money every year on referral commissions, or bird-dogging.

A bird-dog is someone that finds leads and gives them to an experienced investor to work. If the investor buys the house, the bird-dog will receive a fee. I typically ask for $1,000 to $2,000 depending on how much potential I feel the deal has. I think most investors probably pay closer to $500 each if the leads are screened as well as I screen mine.

What I mean by screening is just that I make sure the potential for a deal is really there. The sellers have to have enough equity in the home and there must be signs of motivation to sell. Some investors will pay small fees just for the lead (just giving the lead, whether they buy the house or not). Don't expect very much if this is the case (probably between $25-$50).

My decision to bird-dog a lead has everything to do with the location of the property. If it's in an area I just don't want to be in, I will pass the lead to another investor. However, if the seller is asking a crazy low price, I am much more likely to try to just contract the deal and wholesale it. If they are asking a so-so price, it's an immediate bird-dog.

If the house is in a price range where my 70% percent of ARV means too big of a discount for the sellers but they are willing to accept less of a discount, I will typically bird-dog the lead as well. An example would be a house that has an ARV (after repaired value) of $500k. At 70%, I would need to buy the house for $350k, minus whatever the cost of repairs would be. That's hard to swallow for people who aren't really motivated. If they would be willing to take something around $400k, there's probably an investor willing to do the deal, but it's not me. I'll call up one of the investors I know that buys higher-dollar properties and offer them the lead.

So, how do I make sure I get paid when I bird-dog leads? I get asked this all the time. You could have the investor sign an agreement stating they will pay you the fee if they buy the house. I don't; I just send leads to people who know that if they want to continue getting great leads from me, they are going to do the right thing. Most serious investors will have no problem making sure you get paid.

When deciding who to pass leads on to, only work with investors who move quickly and communicate often. You don't want to have to be chasing these guys down every couple of days to find out if they got the house under contract or when they are closing.

Summary of results

This book covers 34 weeks of recording, tracking, and analyzing leads and making deals. While I detail these deals in the section to come, here is a quick summary of my results. I do this so you can see, at a glance, which marketing tactics work the best and how many leads I had to sift through to find the gems.

Lead source	Number of leads	Number under contract
Buying website	277	7
Bandit signs	71	2
Yellow pages ad	49	0
Absentee owners list	29	1
Drive for dollars	18	0
Wholesalers	18	0
Probate letters	8	2
Realtors, REO and MLS	22	0
Referrals	10	0
FSBO/Craigslist	3	0
Totals	**505**	**11**

Over the course of 34 weeks, I collected 505 leads, 11 of which became deals. They were a combination of wholesale deals and rehab jobs that brought in close to $250,000. This was a result of a lot of work on my part to follow leads, answer the phone any time people call, make offers on almost every house I heard about, and build relationships with Realtors, wholesalers and contractors over the past 10 years.

Flipping houses has allowed me freedom from a 9-to-5 and time to take vacation whenever I want. If you follow the guidelines and patterns throughout this book, there's no reason you can't do well for yourself, too.

Week 1

Motivated Seller Marketing

This week begins the opening up of my records for you guys to see how my wife and I operate our real estate investing business.

Let me mention something upfront. You may notice that I pass up on some deals that other investors would go after. This is because I am only interested in good deals. As I mentioned in the Introduction, I have specific factors I'm looking for and prefer certain types of neighborhoods. I don't want to get busy rehabbing five dumps in war zones and miss the home run deal that would make more than all of those houses combined (and not have to worry about getting mugged in the process). I do make money from some of these junkers, usually in the form of bird-dogging or wholesaling, depending on the price of the house.

I started off this week by putting up some bandit signs (actually, I had my contractor do it) and I am always amazed at how quickly a small investment in these signs produces results. I had a deal that was put under contract within 5 days. It's really that easy.

My tip of the week is to learn how to quickly filter out the non-deals. Don't get caught up in trying to make deals when it's just not going to happen. Usually, you're tempted when you don't have enough leads coming in. Work on getting more leads and get used to saying, "Next!"

Lead Analysis

Lead source	Number of leads
Bandit signs	5
Yellow pages	1
Buying website	1
Drive for dollars	1
Total	**8**

1. Newer House in Older Neighborhood
[Source: Website]

This one was a 3 bedroom, 2 bath newer house built in the middle of a neighborhood of older, run-down houses. Here are the numbers:

- Asking Price: Make an offer
- Amount Owed: $30,000
- Repairs: Unknown
- After Repaired Value: $75,000
- Max Offer: $48,750 (65% of ARV) minus repairs

You can tell there are some gaps in that data. It's because, as you get more leads coming in, you have to be able to filter the time wasters from the true prospects. This seller would not name a price and generally seemed like he just wanted to see if he could get full price. When this happens, I just determine the basics and call back with a ballpark. This really weeds out the non-deals.

Based on what he told me about the condition of the house, I told him I would probably be able to offer somewhere between $40,000 and $45,000 cash. Usually, I am not so conservative when giving the ballparks because I don't want to scare the seller off too easily. If I have to negotiate it down, it is easier done face-to-face with the seller. So, if they really have any motivation at all, they will allow me to come and look at it to give them a firm offer. If they don't, they simply weren't motivated enough. I do call and follow up after a week or so to see if they've thought any more about selling at the lower price.

2. Small House but Decent Area [Hidden Iron House]
[Source: Bandit Signs]

This one is the kind of lead I am looking for. It's a 2 bedroom, 1 bath, 1.5 car garage, 907-square-foot house built in 1995.

Here are the numbers:

- Asking Price: $30,000
- Amount Owed: $5,000 (taxes)
- Repairs: $10,000
- After Repaired Value: $70,000
- Max Offer: $32,000 ($42,000 (60%) - $10,000)

What I like about this one should be obvious. He was asking a very reasonable price from the get-go. He inherited the house and only owes the taxes. He didn't want or need it — this happens a lot with inherited properties — they just don't want to deal with the hassles of selling a house that is not in good shape.

You may have noticed that I chose 60% of ARV for my maximum offer. This was because the house is a small 2/1, which do not sell as well as the standard 3/2. The comps used were 2/1's also, so the ARV is correct. Here, I'm just accounting for longer days on market.

I immediately scheduled to see this property and made an offer of $25,000 on the spot, after walking through it. I did not offer my max allowable offer so I had room to negotiate. You can always go up on your offer, but rarely can you go down. The seller wanted to talk it over with his wife that evening. He called me that night and accepted. I got the house under contract this morning and will close mid-April.

19

In the weeks to come, I'll mention details of this deal. To see final numbers and timeline, find the Hidden Iron House in the Flipped Houses section at the end of the book.

3. Weird Conjoined House
[Source: Bandit Signs]

This property was two houses on separate lots joined together by a previous owner. Both houses had 2 bedrooms and 1 bath, combined for a total of 2300-square-foot with two kitchens. Here are the numbers:

- Asking Price: $65,000
- Amount Owed: $0
- Repairs: Totally gutted
- After Repaired Value: $75,000
- Max Offer: $45,000 minus repairs and $10k wholesale fee

This house was gutted and destroyed by vandals. The seller says the wiring was ripped out of the walls, the sheetrock torn off the studs throughout, and other miscellaneous damage from vandals over the last five years. Due to the hassles with this one, I know I would need to get it super cheap because I would wholesale it to a rehabber that would need it super cheap, so I offered $15,000. He wasn't having it.

4. War Zone Full-Value House
[Source: Bandit Signs]

You will get a lot of calls from people that want to, and in many cases need to, sell their house at full value. This one was in a bad part of town and owed what it was worth. This was quickly determined by the fact that they had just bought the house (with owner financing at 12%) a couple of years ago. You should not spend a lot of time on the phone with these sellers. It's always tempting to try to help them because you feel bad, but there is no realistic way to do that. Do not waste your time or theirs. Get off the phone.

--

I got 4 other leads this week, but none were of particular note. Either they were in bad neighborhoods where I don't invest or the numbers just didn't work out in my favor.

Next Steps

- Get a list of 500 absentee owners.
- Drive for dollars in target neighborhoods.
- Distribute $20 marketing cards everywhere I go.

Week 2

More Marketing

This week, there were quite a few leads, but nothing really great. That just means I am getting closer to the good ones.

I was not able to get the list of absentee owners this week because we switched title companies recently and I had the wrong login information. I am getting in contact with someone to resolve this.

Keep track of all of your leads and deal analysis with FlipPilot. It's what I use to keep track of all my data. Seriously cool. Check it out at flippilot.com

Lead Analysis

Lead source	Number of leads
Bandit signs	4
Yellow pages	2
Buying website	7
Realtors	1
Total	**14**

1. House in Decent Neighborhood
[Source: Bandit Signs]

This one was a 3 bedroom, 2 bath, 1200-square-foot house that was built in 1984.

Here are the numbers:

- Asking Price: $60,000
- Amount Owed: $46,000
- Repairs: Unknown
- After Repaired Value: $75,000
- Max Offer: $48,750 (65% of ARV) minus repairs

With this one, based on what she told me about the condition of the house, I would need to get it for no more than about $40,000. They owe more than that and are not behind on payments. I don't usually do short sales anyway, as they are just too much work. This is the type of deal that some people are tempted to try and make work because if you just bend your criteria a little, you can squeeze enough profit out to make it a "deal." Don't do it; move on to the next one.

2. House in Neighborhood Next to The Last One
[Source: Website]

This one was also a 3 bedroom, 2 bath, 1300-square-foot house that was built in 1984.

Here are the numbers:

- Asking Price: $85,000
- Amount Owed: $45,000
- Repairs: $10,000 (estimated from listing pictures)
- After Repaired Value: $90,000
- Max Offer: $48,500 ($58,500 (65% of ARV) - $10,000)

This one was listed on MLS. I was able to see pictures and make a rough estimate of the repair costs. The seller is out of state, which gave me a reason to see if he would consider such a low offer. He wasn't interested and I thought he was starting to go into the "you're trying to steal the house speech," but he didn't. Turned out to be a nice guy, but was not willing to go below $75k. I will follow up to see what he does.

3. House Backs Up to Busy Road
[Source: REO]

The listing agent called me on this 4 bedroom, 1 bath, converted garage, 1200-square-foot house.

Here are the numbers:

- Asking Price: $56,000
- Amount Owed: $0
- Repairs: $14,000
- After Repaired Value: $90,000
- Max Offer: $40,000 (60% ARV minus $14k for repairs)

The problem with this house is that it backs up to a busy road (reason for the 60% used for maximum offer calculation) and the house was just hideous. This really does affect resale value and needs to be taken into account when figuring out numbers. Another thing to watch out for is junkie neighbors, which really affects how quickly a house will sell. I don't know how many times I've ignored this and my wife has chewed me out upon arriving to see this "great deal" for the first time.

4. Pre-Foreclosure
[Source: Website]

This one was a 3 bedroom, 2.5 bath, 2000-square-foot house that is facing foreclosure. This house is only 6 years old.

Danny Johnson

Here are the numbers:

- Asking Price: $115,000
- Amount Owed: $115,000
- Repairs: Few cosmetic
- After Repaired Value: $120,000
- Max Offer: $78,000 minus repairs

I took this call while helping my brother move. Always take your calls. Don't be like your competition — actually pick up your phone when people call you and you'll stand out.

This is not a deal for me because of what is owed and the fact that the house does not really need repairs. I've done some, but really would rather not spend much time on them. (Do you see a trend here? No, not laziness.)

--

I got 10 other leads this week, but none were very good. A few just didn't have the numbers while most were in terrible neighborhoods and I just wasn't interested.

Week 3

Leads and Deal Analysis

This week I got some pretty good leads, but none are under contract. At the time, I thought a few might pan out, but it didn't turn out that way.

I'm also still working on getting the absentee owner list and should have something early next week. I ordered 200 more bandit signs from supercheapsigns.com.

Lead Analysis

Lead source	Number of leads
Bandit signs	2
Yellow pages	1
Buying website	9
Referral	1
Total	**14**

1. Good Central Location
[Source: Website]

This house is a 3 bedroom, 2 bath, 1200-square-foot house that was built in 1955.

Here are the numbers:

- Asking Price: Make an offer
- Amount Owed: $0

- Repairs: $23,000
- After Repaired Value: $85,000
- Max Offer: $32,000 ($55k - $23k repairs)

This house is one that I am interested in. It does require a lot of repairs, but I feel it would sell very quickly once finished. It is most definitely the ugliest house on the street (this is what you want). The owner lives out of town and has talked with other investors, so I offered close to my max ($30,000) with a quick closing and he said he would call me.

This is where you need to try to get them to make a faster decision so that they don't go and call a thousand other investors. Some will no matter what, so you don't want to force the matter. Just politely request that they inform you soon because you are looking at several properties and need to know where your funds are going to be allocated. I will call him soon to follow up if I don't hear from him.

2. Duplex Near Our Old House
[Source: Website]

This house is a 1910 duplex with 1/1 on each side.

Here are the numbers:

- Asking Price: $30,000
- Amount Owed: $0
- Repairs: $40,000
- After Repaired Value: $90,000
- Max Offer: $14,000 ($54k [60% ARV because of the amount of work] - $40k repairs)

This house is actually near where we used to live. My wife and I bought a run-down historic house and rehabbed the whole thing. It had been vacant for about 20+ years and sort of had the whole fight-club-paper-street house thing going on. We finished the inside and moved in, but the outside was still a wreck.

One time, my wife and a friend went downtown for a ladies' night out. They took a cab home and the driver kept asking, "Are you sure you want to be dropped off here? This house?" It looked like a giant vagrant-filled dump.

Anyway, this house (the lead) needs a ton of work. Everything from the roller-coaster foundation to the gas water heater with no vent in the kitchen. Oh, did I mention the fire that burned the back bedroom completely?

I made the offer but they are sort of delusional about the value of the place as they were told by someone that the lot was worth $75k+.

The lesson to take away from this one is that the seller was visibly embarrassed about the state of the house. In these situations, you really do need to make sure to only mention the potential the house has and that you know how hard it is to keep up an old house. Do not rip the house apart; have sympathy.

3. Small House with Central Location
[Source: Website]

This house is a 2 bed, 1 bath, 900-square-foot house.

Here are the numbers:

- Asking Price: $25,000 then mentioned $20,000
- Amount Owed: $22,000
- Repairs: Unknown
- After Repaired Value: $40,000
- Max Offer: $15,000 minus repairs

If you noticed, I mentioned the seller was willing to consider taking less than what they owe. They would have to come to the table with money or convince the lender to take less. That spells motivated to me. It's a shame the area is not better. I passed this one on to see if someone could make a deal out of it.

4. Property Saved from Foreclosure
[Source: Website]

This house is a 3 bedroom, 2 bath, 1600-square-foot house built in 1986, and this one has the smell of money.

Here are the numbers:

- Asking Price: Make an offer (okay because situation is ripe for good price)
- Amount Owed: $900
- Repairs: Unknown
- After Repaired Value: $100,000
- Max Offer: $65,000 minus repairs

This is a couple of doors down from a house we did a few years ago. That is one of the things I love about this business. We can drive around in most parts of the city and point out properties we have done. It doesn't seem like a whole lot when you are doing them, but it really adds up — especially in the neighborhoods we like.

The seller of this house lives out of town and saved the house from foreclosure for his ex-girlfriend. I've never had this situation before, but it represents a good opportunity. I'll likely be seeing this one next week.

5. Foreclosure with a Pool
[Source: REO]

This house is a 3 bedroom, 2 bath, 1700-square-foot house built in 1960 and has a converted garage.

Here are the numbers:

- Asking Price: $117,000
- Amount Owed: $0 — bank-owned
- Repairs: $35,000 (this place needs everything)
- After Repaired Value: $155,000
- Max Offer: $65,000

This bank-owned home has a pool that has not been taken care of. I guess you could say the whole house wasn't taken care of. It needs new kitchen cabinets, countertops, appliances, sheetrock repair, painting, flooring, light fixtures, new HVAC, pool work, new doors, new flooring and demo.

I've offered quite a bit below asking price ($60k). Don't be afraid to do that with bank-owned properties. If you are building a relationship with an REO Realtor, you don't want to make them submit an offer this low if the house was just listed or they tell you it is a waste of time. Do not waste their time. If a Realtor calls you with a deal, try to drop everything and head over and then get back to them as soon as possible. If you hustle, even if you don't buy the property, you increase your chances of them calling you with another house. However, don't try to make a deal out of a non-deal just to build a relationship with a Realtor. If you go out of business, your relationship won't matter one bit.

My offer was not accepted, but I will keep an eye on this one.

6. Facing Foreclosure
[Source: Website]

This house is a 3 bedroom, 2 bath, 1700-square-foot house built in 1977.

Here are the numbers:

- Asking Price: $137,000 (but know they won't get that)
- Amount Owed: $77,000
- Repairs: Cosmetic
- After Repaired Value: $140,000
- Max Offer: $91,000 minus repairs

The sellers are facing foreclosure, but say they have to ability to avoid it. They just want to see about selling it and collecting some of their equity. Not sure why they let it go into foreclosure if they have money to make the payments.

I told them I would give them a ballpark because I am still trying to feel them out for their level of motivation. I would probably be in the 80's depending on repairs. They weren't interested right away, but this is worth following up on. Time tends to change people's minds.

--

This week, I got 7 other leads that were not really worth mentioning. Primarily, the numbers just didn't work out or the locations weren't great for me.

Week 4

Absentee Owners List

This week, I didn't get to fly to Carlsbad Caverns because of 35+ mph surface winds that do not bode well for small airplanes. I wasn't really phased though, as I also got the best news this week: I am going to be a dad again! My wife and I have 4 beautiful girls and now we are expecting another (maybe a boy... not that I wouldn't be happy with another a girl).

I also had lunch with one of the top REO agents in San Antonio on Tuesday. We had a great time and got to hear some good stories. I also did an interview with her, where we talk about how to contact and deal with REO agents. This will be a great way for people to see the other point of view. You can download and listen to it at flippingjunkie.com/interview-with-a-top-reo-agent

I have been bird-dogging a lot out the last few weeks. So far, three are under contract and I will get paid finder's fees for each when they close. One of them is supposed to pay $5k.

Lead Analysis

Lead source	Number of leads
Bandit signs	3
Yellow pages	2
Buying website	4
Total	**9**

1. Investor Selling As-Is

[Source: Bandit Signs]

This investor wants to get rid of a 3 bedroom, 2 bath house that he has partially rehabbed.

Here are the numbers:

- Asking Price: $57,000
- Amount Owed: $0
- Repairs: Complete rehab — probably about $20k.
- After Repaired Value: $80,000
- Max Offer: $48,000 minus repairs

This case was an investor trying to find the greater fool. There is no way I would buy this house anywhere near his asking price, even if it didn't need as many repairs as I am guessing. Keep this in mind when you're gathering leads: your competitors are trying to make money too.

2. Great Wholesale
[Source: Bandit Signs]

This is a homeowner selling a 2 bedroom, 1 bath, 1200-square-foot house, built 1950.

Here are the numbers:

- Asking Price: $12,000 — gotta love reasonable asking prices
- Amount Owed: $0 (some back taxes)
- Repairs: Unknown
- After Repaired Value: $45,000
- Max Offer: $20,000 minus repairs

This is an inherited house that needs repairs. The neighborhood is a rough one but I'm sure I could wholesale it.

3. Bad Neighborhood — House Looks Decent on Google
[Source: Website]

This house is a 3 bedroom, 2 bath, 1400-square-foot house that was built in 1956.

Here are the numbers:

- Asking Price: $20,000
- Amount Owed: $0
- Repairs: Unknown
- After Repaired Value: $50,000
- Max Offer: Not for me

Another inherited house. This one is in a neighborhood that I do not buy in. The seller is asking a reasonable price and this one is going to my go-to guy. He can probably work it and give me something for my referral.

4. Wanting to Move Overseas
[Source: Yellow Pages]

This house is a 3 bedroom, 2 bath, 1200-square-foot house that was built in 1951.

Here are the numbers:

- Asking Price: $75,000
- Amount Owed: $0
- Repairs: Minor repairs
- After Repaired Value: $90,000
- Max Offer: $58,000 (65% ARV minus repairs)

I made a ballpark of about $50,000 on this one because they did not seem at all motivated. They will call me if they decide that number is reasonable for them. A note to follow up with them is already in my planner.

--

This week I got 4 other leads, including a PO Box. Most were just average houses and didn't have the numbers to become deals for me, so I bird-dogged them.

Week 5

Now with More Fleas!

With it warming up, the fleas are getting out of control again. I don't know what causes it, but a house can have a pet with fleas and they don't seem to take over, then as soon as that house goes vacant, they multiply like crazy and there are billions of them. Shouldn't be a big deal though as most people like fleas, right?

This week, I found addresses for the driving for dollars houses from the other week. The ugliest and most obviously long-time vacant properties get a star marked next to the address — these are the ones that I am not only going to send letters to, but I will track down phone numbers and call if possible.

I also had 50 more bandit signs put out. I was livid when I drove through the area and saw that they were all put along roads far away from any intersections. This guy had put them out before and put them exactly as I had told him (at intersections, you know, where people are actually stopped and have time to write down the number or dial it…) He got an earful from me. As I drove to view a couple properties this week, I saw some more of them and had to laugh at how awful it was that I just barely caught a glimpse of them as I drove 45 mph past them. Oh well. Good thing I checked on his placement of the signs. I think the number of calls from signs this week reflects the poor placement.

We closed on the house I put under contract in Week 1. Again, you can find information about this house (Hidden Iron House) in the Flipped Houses section at the end of the book.

Overall, I've been making a decent amount of offers and nothing has been sticking. It is important to understand that this will happen. You will always have flat spots where nothing seems to be working and then all of a sudden you will get a flood of sellers accepting your offers. Sometimes the sellers you've made offers to months ago will call and want to deal too. Keep the faith; don't let this discourage you.

If you're just starting out, you might be interested in an article I wrote about the top five things to do when getting started flipping houses. You can find it online at http://www.flippingjunkie.com/?p=541

Lead Analysis

Lead source	Number of leads
Bandit signs	3
Buying website	6
Drive for dollars	5
REO	2
Wholesale	1
Total	**17**

1. Neighborhood I Know Well
[Source: Drive for Dollars]

This homeowner wants to get rid of a 3 bedroom, 1 bath house that is vacant.

Here are the numbers:

- Asking Price: $65,000
- Amount Owed: $0
- Repairs: $18,000
- After Repaired Value: $95,000
- Max Offer: $44,000 (65% of ARV - $18,000)

The house needs a lot of repairs and the seller wants to sell because he has remarried and moved to another house. He has a choice to fix up this house or work on the hot rods that he owns. Which would you choose? I hope you said the house.

He is hung up on $65k, but I could only offer him $40k. I will definitely follow up with him as I know he wants to work on those cars.

2. You've Gotta Be Kiddin' Me
[Source: Website]

This homeowner called with a 3 bedroom, 2 bath house in a suburb of San Antonio.

Here are the numbers:

- Asking Price: $89,000
- Amount Owed: $89,000
- Repairs: Mostly cosmetic
- After Repaired Value: $110,000
- Max Offer: $71,000 minus repairs

The seller wants to move back to Dallas but owes too much on the house. When I mentioned having to buy it for around $70k, I could hear the husband in the background saying "You've gotta be kiddin' me!" Not gonna do it.

3. Probate Deal from Drive for Dollars
[Source: Drive for Dollars]

A homeowner called with a 3 bedroom, 2 bath house in an area close to my house.

Here are the numbers:

- Asking Price: Make an offer
- Amount Owed: $0

- Repairs: $20,000
- After Repaired Value: $105,000
- Max Offer: $48,000 ($68,000 - $20,000 repairs)

Executrix of the estate called me from a letter we sent. The deceased was a hoarder and they are in the process of cleaning out the house. First, I told them to stop cleaning it out. I will buy it with all the junk in it and save them the hassle. They said they were in the middle of probate and were going to be there the next day. I went to see it and offered $42,000.

When I called to follow up on my offer, they informed me that two of the heirs were complaining that the offer was low and they felt they could get more. This always happens when there is more than one heir! Two more investors were coming to make an offer on Saturday. The only thing to do here is be polite and tell them to call after the others have made their offers to see what you can do.

The power of envisioning what you want truly works. I was focusing my thoughts on getting this one throughout the day yesterday. This morning (before I even got up) they called me. The executrix informed me that they'd had a conference call and decided to do the deal for $45k. More on this story in the coming weeks.

4. Lost Job
[Source: Bandit Signs]

This homeowner called with a 4 bedroom, 2 bath house in a good area.

Here are the numbers:

- Asking Price: $195,000
- Amount Owed: $136,000 (first $128k, second $8k)
- Repairs: Unknown (they say no repairs are needed — I've heard that before...)
- After Repaired Value: $220,000
- Max Offer: $143,000 minus repairs

I took this call in my new (used) car with Bluetooth link up to my phone. My wife was with me and was able to take down the information as I was asking the seller questions. It's much nicer than when I would have her hold the phone while I asked the questions and then she'd have to try to write while holding the phone or me driving, talking on the phone and repeating everything the seller says. Gotta love technology.

I'd probably need to get this for no more than what is owed. He did not sound very interested in my ballpark of around $150k less repairs. I will call him in a week or so and see how he is doing.

5. Small REO in Decent Area
[Source: REO]

An REO agent called with a 2 bedroom, 1 bath house in a blah area.

Here are the numbers:

- Asking Price: $14,000
- Amount Owed: $0
- Repairs: $20,000
- After Repaired Value: $55,000
- Max Offer: $10,000

This is the time of year that I dread going into nasty houses: fleas! I hate those darn little things that you don't even notice until you have been back in your car for five minutes and see that you are covered in them. Then comes the dance in the middle of the street trying to get them all off because you don't want to bring any of them home with you. Luckily, there were only about five of them on me today.

This is a great neighborhood for selling with owner financing but not so much for selling retail. I'm really not interested in this property, but will make an offer anyway and see what happens. I'll attempt to wholesale if I get it under contract.

6. Crispy Burn House
[Source: Drive for Dollars]

I called the homeowner of this badly burned 3 bedroom, 2 bath house in a good area.

Here are the numbers:

- Asking Price: Wasn't going to sell but now might consider it
- Amount Owed: $0
- Repairs: $60,000+
- After Repaired Value: $125,000
- Max Offer: $15,000 ($75k - $60k)

This was a property my wife and I saw while driving for dollars the other week. It had a roll-off dumpster in front that looked like it was filled months ago. Nothing was happening at the house and there was a code compliance notice posted on the door. I found the owner's name from the county appraisal district's website and then found his phone number in the white pages.

He told me he was getting estimates from contractors but was not having an easy time. Contractors usually don't make for easy times. I told him we might be interested in buying it and that I would make him an offer if he would consider selling it. I'll follow up to see if he changes his mind about doing all that work to fix the place up.

7. Property Already Under Contract
[Source: Bandit Signs]

A homeowner called with a 3 bedroom, 2 bath house in a not-so-good area.

Here are the numbers:

- Asking Price: $45k down to $40k
- Amount Owed: $26,000
- Repairs: Unknown

- After Repaired Value: $70,000
- Max Offer: $45,000 (65% ARV minus repairs)

The homeowner called from a sign and mentioned that she already has it under contract but that it had been well over a month with a lock box on the house. After a little digging, I found out that another investor is trying to wholesale it and is dragging it out because they cannot find a buyer. She was not sure of the closing date on the contract, but I need to find out if it has expired. If not, the next step is to call the title company and see if it was ever receipted with earnest money.

8. Wholesale House
[Source: Wholesaler]

A wholesaler called with a 3 bedroom, 2 bath, 1000-square-foot house in an okay area.

Here are the numbers:

- Asking Price: $48,000
- Amount Owed: Unknown
- Repairs: $8,000
- After Repaired Value: $78,000
- Max Offer: $50,000 minus repairs

The days on market are pretty high for this house and nothing has sold in the immediate area in a while. The ones that sold last year were rehabbed very nicely (read: more expensive than what I would do). I called and said I would have to buy for close to $40k depending on actual repair numbers. I did this before going out there because I am not going to waste my time until there is room to have the wholesaler come down on his price. This is just where the numbers are at for me.

--

In addition to these leads, I got nine others this week that weren't great. Mostly, the numbers just wouldn't work, especially when the owners owe too much. And again, I got a bunch in neighborhoods I'm not interested in.

Week 6

Getting Chewed Out

I'm still negotiating with the seller on the deal from last week. She lives an hour away and does not have transportation, so I faxed an agreement with the agreed to price to her. I really should have just driven to her and had it taken care of. I've followed up for three days and she finally called this morning to tell me she was taking it to her attorney.

I hate when they do that because attorneys usually try to negotiate the deal instead of verifying the legality of the agreement — this was mentioned to the seller in hopes that she would not call back with demands.

Well, she did...several times. I ended up having to pay more earnest money and the title policy. When I get home, the signed agreement is on my fax machine and now includes me paying all closing costs. No way!

I immediately called and talked it over. They are not budging, so I informed her that I needed to look at the house again. My gut was telling me to re-check comparable sales too.

You really need to listen to your gut in these situations. Mine is starting to tell me it is no longer a deal. The biggest thing to learn here is to try and stay in control of your deals. I should have driven the agreement to her and had her sign it as soon as we agreed over the phone. You should always be willing to walk away from a deal. I'm not going to try to make this a deal if it isn't one. Sometimes, it can be hard to walk away from one that is so close, but you have to stick to your numbers. You get into trouble down the road when you don't. If I don't buy, I will try and make sure it's someone I know that does.

I'm also trying to put another one under contract — and I closed another one this week, but it was one I had put under contract before starting this book. It will not be included here as I only want to record what I've gotten from these 34 weeks.

Lead Analysis

Lead source	Number of leads
Bandit signs	5
Yellow pages	1
Buying website	4
Wholesale	1
Absentee owners	2
Total	**13**

1. Divorce Situation
[Source: Yellow Pages]

This homeowner wants to get rid of a 3 bedroom, 2 bath house with a partially converted garage, built in 2004.

Here are the numbers:

- Asking Price: What is owed plus something
- Amount Owed: $64,000
- Repairs: Unknown
- After Repaired Value: $80,000
- Max Offer: $52,000 minus repairs

The seller cannot afford the house payments. This seems to happen a lot with divorce situations where they could afford the house with two incomes, but cannot with just one. She mentioned that the garage conversion was never completed. This is a newer house that was built in a junky older neighborhood when the real estate market was really heating up. Not such a good buy now. Too much is owed and I feel this would be pretty hard to sell.

2. Works for Government and Transferred
[Source: Website]

A homeowner wants to get rid of a 3 bedroom, 2.5 bath house built in 2001 in a newer neighborhood.

Here are the numbers:

- Asking Price: $106,000 (then down to $70,000 when asked least they would take!)
- Amount Owed: $68,000
- Repairs: Unknown
- After Repaired Value: $100,000
- Max Offer: $65,000 minus repairs

This one is in an area that I really don't like to buy in. Days on market is high and there are a lot of foreclosures to compete with. Add that they owe just over what I want to buy it for and I just don't want to do it. I'm sure another investor will be interested, so I passed this one on.

3. Giant Historic House
[Source: Bandit Signs]

This homeowner is facing foreclosure and needs to sell a 5 bedroom, 2.5 bath, 4300-square-foot house in a historic neighborhood.

Here are the numbers:

- Asking Price: $300,000
- Amount Owed: $275,000
- Repairs: Unknown
- After Repaired Value: $350,000-400,000 (depends on the quality of the rehab)
- Max Offer: $225,000 minus repairs

This house will be up for auction, and I heard about it just 7 days before. This is a lot of money to scrape together that fast. I love these older houses,

47

but they can be huge money pits. By the way, if you have never seen *Money Pit* with Tom Hanks, you really should.

This house faces a very busy road and it makes me question my ARV. This would only work if the foreclosure was postponed and a short sale worked out. The work involved to even try it is keeping me from wanting to do this deal; too much risk.

4. Rental Property With 8 Year Tenant
[Source: Absentee Owner Mailing]

This landlord has a 4 bedroom, 2 bath, 2000-square-foot house they *might* sell.

Here are the numbers:

- Asking Price: Make an offer — strike one
- Amount Owed: Unknown; wouldn't say — strike two
- Repairs: Maybe a roof
- After Repaired Value: $145,000
- Max Offer: $94,000 (65% ARV minus repairs)

This one came through the absentee owner mailing. The issue with this type of marketing is that you will get a lot of unmotivated sellers calling you. This one is a tire kicker and I did not spend a lot of time analyzing the lead. I gave a ballpark in the 80's and they were not even remotely interested. Their tenant has paid religiously for 8 years, so they don't need to sell.

--

The 9 other leads I got this week were primarily in bad neighborhoods or simply bad deals. In addition to the one mentioned above, I bird-dogged four of them, including one to my dad to see if they could make it work.

Active deals

Hidden Iron House

I closed on this house last week and already have my contractor started on the repairs. I got my contractor to give me a bid and also found a new contractor to quote me. The new contractor came in over twice what my contractor said. He asked if I wanted him to fax it over and I told him not to bother. He immediately came down half. My guy is getting the job and this guy knows to give me a good estimate next time.

My guy is doing the work for about $4,000. You can find details of the scope of work in the Flipped Houses section.

Next steps

- Call more REO Realtors.
- Check on rehabs.
- Get probate leads from the courthouse.

Week 7

Twenty-One Leads

What do I have to do to put another one under contract? I know the next one will come soon as I've had lots of leads. The absentee owner leads really stink. Now I remember why I haven't sent them in a long time!

I backed out of the one where the attorney was re-negotiating terms. If they call me back and agree to my offer, I will accept, but I will not accept their new terms. They said they have two other people interested, but I have to stick to my guns and not cross the maximum offer line that I calculated for myself. Sometimes this is very hard to do, but do it we must.

If you're struggling with your bookkeeping, my wife wrote an article this week that might help you out. You can find it online at http://www.flippingjunkie.com/?p=726

Lead Analysis

Lead source	Number of leads
Bandit signs	10
Yellow pages	2
Buying website	2
REO, Realtors, MLS	4
Absentee owners	3
Total	**21**

1. Realtor Owned Fixer
[Source: Bandit Signs]

This Realtor/owner wants to sell a 3 bedroom, 1.5 bath, vacant house that needs quite a bit of work.

Here are the numbers:

- Asking Price: $55,000
- Amount Owed: Unknown
- Repairs: $20,000+
- After Repaired Value: $80,000
- Max Offer: $28,000 ($48,000 - $20,000 in repairs)

This is a case where a Realtor came across a good deal and snatched it up in hopes to sell it for profit. It needs quite a bit of work and it's hard to get a good idea of the ARV on this house because the neighborhood has 'pockets' (differing areas street by street). Comps showed a little higher, but the square footage this house had was mostly in a garage conversion and a very poorly done back porch enclosure. Be very careful with additions to houses. If they were done poorly and not up to code, you should deduct from the after repaired value rather than increase it for the extra square footage.

2. My Realtor Stinks
[Source: Yellow Pages]

A homeowner wants to sell a 3 bedroom, 2 bath house in a neighborhood I've bought a lot of houses in.

Here are the numbers:

- Asking Price: $95,700
- Amount Owed: 22,000
- Repairs: Unknown (cosmetic — unconfirmed)
- After Repaired Value: $105,000
- Max Offer: $68,000 minus repairs

The seller inherited this house and is living in it. He was complaining about how his Realtor was not doing anything. "No showings, no nothin'." Then I found out why: he seems to have a seriously warped opinion of what the house is worth. His idea is that it is worth at least 50% more than it really is. I told him I usually buy in his neighborhood in the 40's and 50's and he did not seem too keen on it. Actually, not at all.

3. I'm Sick of Taking Care of the House
[Source: Yellow Pages]

This homeowner wants to sell a 3 bedroom, 1 bath, 800-square-foot house in a not-so-good area.

Here are the numbers:

- Asking Price: Make an offer
- Amount Owed: Nothing
- Repairs: Foundation repair and other (unconfirmed)
- After Repaired Value: $55,000
- Max Offer: $30,000 minus repairs

The seller is a son who is tired of taking care of his mother's house. She is the owner and is still alive. He is trying to get an idea on price, but I am going to pass this on in hopes of getting a bird-dog fee because I don't like the area. Ones like this I am tempted to try and buy to wholesale, but I make a decent amount when bird-dogging and for a lot less work. Plus, some of the people I pass on to are able to make lemonade out of lemons.

4. My Ex Offered Me X Amount
[Source: Bandit Signs]

This homeowner wants to sell a 3 bedroom, 2 bath, 1100-square-foot house in a decent neighborhood.

Here are the numbers:

- Asking Price: $90,000
- Amount Owed: $65,000
- Repairs: Says a lot
- After Repaired Value: $95,000
- Max Offer: $61,000 minus repairs

I like this neighborhood because I sold a house very fast here last year. It's too bad the owner owes too much and is stuck on her outrageous price. The house needs a lot of work (according to her) and she owes $65k and says her ex-husband offered $20k over that. She wants $5k more than his offer and there is no way I will ever be able to do that. Next.

5. Listed Fixer
[Source: MLS]

This one is a vacant 4 bedroom, 2 bath, 1100-square-foot house, built in the 70's.

Here are the numbers:

- Asking Price: $60,000
- Amount Owed: $0 (REO)
- Repairs: $20,000
- After Repaired Value: $85,000
- Max Offer: $31,000 (60% ARV minus repairs)

This house is a true piece of junk and the neighbors are a little junky (which is why I've done the numbers with 60% of ARV instead of my usual 65%). The house has settling issues and the owner looks to have just quickly patched and painted over the cracks. Another low ball. I try to make an offer on every house I look at, even if I don't want it. If I don't want it, I just offer lower in order to be able to wholesale it. If you spend time looking at a house, you should make an offer, even if it's ridiculous. Don't let your time go to waste; you never know what somebody will accept.

--

Of the 16 other leads from this week, most were just unmotivated sellers that I couldn't make deals with. I bird-dogged a few as well.

Active deals

Hidden Iron House
The house I got under contract in Week 1 is now complete and on the market. Find more details about the final numbers, timeline and work involved in the Flipped Houses section.

You'll also find photos at
http://flippingjunkie.com/hidden-iron-house-for-sale

Next steps
- Get another one under contract.
- Call more REO Realtors.
- Check on rehabs.
- Get more probate leads from the courthouse and send letters.
- Have more bandit signs put out.
- If there's time, I'll do another drive for dollars.

Week 8

Another Twenty-Three Leads

My family has been dealing with a cold all week. Not fun. I stop for nothing, though. I still analyzed 23 leads and did some marketing.

I only got 25 bandit signs up before code compliance decided to finally call and set me straight. I will wait a couple of weeks and put out some more in a different area.

I also got another angry call. In fact, this guy was so angry he called several times *and* paged me. I called back to get an earful for a couple of minutes. It was from a probate letter and I completely understand where he was coming from. Some people do find this approach insensitive. Of course, this doesn't justify calling someone and yelling at them, but I understand it. You have to be ready for these types of calls when you mail to probate; they are guaranteed.

I'm finding the website is bringing in tons of leads for me — mostly decent ones. If you'd like a website like mine, you can get one at http://leadpropeller.com/flippinghousesexposed

Managing leads when you start to get this many can be a daunting task. I've developed software that allows you to keep track of your leads, set up follow-up reminders, do deal analysis and all sorts of other awesome things...and it's all accessible on your mobile device! Find out more at flippilot.com

Lead Analysis

Lead source	Number of leads
Bandit signs	4
Yellow pages	2
Buying website	14
Drive for dollars	1
REO	1
Probate	1
Total	**23**

1. Tiny, Tiny House
[Source: Website]

This homeowner wants to sell a 2 bedroom, 1 bath, 600-square-foot house.

Here are the numbers:

- Asking Price: $35,000
- Amount Owed: $0
- Repairs: Cosmetic (unconfirmed)
- After Repaired Value: $50,000
- Max Offer: $25,000 minus repairs

The seller is having a baby and needs a bigger house. They have received an offer from another investor for $30k but want $35k. I wouldn't want it for more than about $20k. Pass.

Tiny houses are hard to sell and this one is in a neighborhood with very, very long days on market. This property would be good to sell with owner financing, but I would still need to get for around $20k.

2. Big Historic House [Historic House]
[Source: Probate Letter]

A homeowner wants to sell a house with 4 bedrooms, 2 baths, and 2700-square-feet that was built in 1939 in a historic neighborhood.

Here are the numbers:

- Asking Price: Make an offer
- Amount Owed: $0
- Repairs: $60,000 roughly
- After Repaired Value: $250,000
- Max Offer: $100,000

The house is vacant and is already being worked on. The kitchen still needs complete updating, the wiring needs updating and the pool needs work. With these houses, the repairs can double very quickly, so this will be a wholesale for me. I offered $90k.

I'll keep you updated on how this deal went in the coming weeks. Find more information about this deal and the final numbers and timeline under Historic House in the Flipped Houses section at the end of the book.

3. Old House with Family of 5 in Attached 1BR Apartment
[Source: Yellow Pages]

The homeowner wants to sell a 3 bedroom, 1 bath, 933-square-foot house built in 1936 with a garage apartment.

Here are the numbers:

- Asking Price: Make an offer
- Amount Owed: $0
- Repairs: Unknown
- After Repaired Value: $70,000
- Max Offer: $40,000 minus repairs

The seller's son is moving out of the house. There is a garage apartment, which is tiny and has a family of 5 living there for $350/mo. The house needs work.

I've scheduled to see the house on Saturday morning. This business doesn't stop at 5 on weekdays. In fact, I took a call for a lead at 10:00 last night. Saturday was the earliest she could show it. She seemed to be somewhat motivated, so I am going to go and see if the house has any potential.

4. Decent Newer House
[Source: REO]

This is a bank-owned 3 bedroom, 2.5 bath, 2200-square-foot house built in 1998 in an area I don't care for.

Here are the numbers:

- Asking Price: $80,000
- Amount Owed: $0
- Repairs: $5,000 (paint and carpet)
- After Repaired Value: $115,000
- Max Offer: $70,000

I don't care much for this area because there are a lot of newer house foreclosures affecting resale values. It is sometimes hard to compete with bank owned properties that are priced great for homeowners that need very little. I offered $67k, but this is a new listing and chances are pretty slim.

5. I Got Really Excited About This One
[Source: Website]

This homeowner wants to sell a 1 bedroom, 1 bath, 1000-square-foot, house *on an airport*.

Here are the numbers:

- Asking Price: $79,000
- Amount Owed: $0
- Repairs: None
- After Repaired Value: Unknown
- Max Offer: Unsure

I'm excited and confused about this one. I would love to own a house on an acre in a flying community where you can taxi out to the runway. The problem is there are no comparables and the house does not have a hangar. What I'll have to do is calculate how much I would need to buy this for to make it a rental. That way, I can make money on it until I decide what I want to do with it. The seller did mention that everybody wants to rent it, but he doesn't want to be a landlord. More on this in the weeks to come.

6. Another Oldie
[Source: Website]

The homeowner wants to sell a 4 bedroom, 3 bath, 1500-square-foot (not sure how that is possible) house in a good owner financing neighborhood.

Here are the numbers:

- Asking Price: $60,000
- Amount Owed: $0
- Repairs: Unknown
- After Repaired Value: $69,000
- Max Offer: $39,000 minus repairs

This is an inherited house owned by someone who lives out of town. The house is currently rented for $500/mo to the same tenant for 10 years. This is a very old house and I'm sure it needs repairs.

--

Most of the 17 other leads from this week just didn't have the numbers I'd need to make it work. Either the sellers wouldn't come down in price or they simply owed too much for it to be worthwhile for me. On to next week!

Next steps

- Make lots of offers.
- Send letters for new our drive for dollars addresses.
- Send more probate letters.

Week 9

A Deal Is Born

Last week, I made a pretty low offer on the house that is on an airport. He didn't take it and said he had higher offers. He called back yesterday and left a message to call him. I thought this was going to be another situation where they call back accepting your offer after some reflection. Instead, he asked me if I knew 'Billy' (real name kept secret), another investor in town. He said 'Billy' had offered much more than everyone else and he could not get a hold of him now. This is typical. It's easy for someone to spout off a number, but when it comes time to follow through, they fall apart and disappear. Please do your homework *before* making an offer. After he gives up on trying to track down this maker of bad offers, he can call me. Who knows. I'm not going to wait around, but if he does call and wants my offer, you can be sure that I will be confident in driving to meet him and signing it up right away.

This week I flew with one of our lenders to Abilene to see some of the properties he is working on up there. He's a pilot and I wanted to go just to go flying. That is one of the best things about being your own boss and setting your own hours. The fact that I was able to get a call this morning and then end up running out to the airport and taking the day off really makes everything worthwhile. We did end up getting stranded out of town about an hour away due to weather, though.

Not as many leads this week, but I did get one under contract, so this is a better week than the last one.

Lead Analysis

Lead source	Number of leads
Yellow pages	1
Buying website	9
Total	**10**

1. Another Separation Situation
[Source: Website]

This homeowner wants to sell a 3 bedroom, 2.5 bath, 1000-square-foot house.

Here are the numbers:

- Asking Price: Make an offer
- Amount Owed: $53,000
- Repairs: Not much — cosmetic (unconfirmed)
- After Repaired Value: $90,000
- Max Offer: $59,000 minus repairs

The seller wants to sell because she is separating from her partner. If the house does, in fact, need just minimal cosmetic repairs, I might be able to buy this. I told them I would probably be buying right above what they owe. She was really anxious about getting rid of the house, but said she would have to think about it as she had hoped to get a lot more.

2. New Construction in Bad Area
[Source: Website]

A homeowner wants to sell a 3 bedroom, 2 bath, 1300-square-foot house built in 2009.

Here are the numbers:

- Asking Price: $60,000
- Amount Owed: $0

- Repairs: Cosmetic (unconfirmed)
- After Repaired Value: $69,000 owner financed
- Max Offer: $35,000 minus repairs

The seller needs money and wants to sell this house. Sounds like a good house, but its location is not so good. This might make a good owner-financed house (sell side) if it barely needs any repairs. I told him my offer would be in the 30's.

3. Small House Weird Situation
[Source: Website]

A homeowner wants to sell a 3 bedroom, 1 bath, 850-square-foot house.

Here are the numbers:

- Asking Price: I'm confused
- Amount Owed: $53,000
- Repairs: Cosmetic (unconfirmed)
- After Repaired Value: $70,000
- Max Offer: $45,000 minus repairs

The caller was not the seller, but calling on behalf of the sellers. He put me on speakerphone and I had to ask them to repeat everything ten times because I could not understand them. Very annoying.

This was a weird situation and I'm not sure if I fully understand. The sellers bought the house to allow the person living there to remain in the house as they were getting foreclosed on. Now, the sellers are paying $1,500/mo for this house and cannot afford it. The person they are trying to keep in the house is not paying and they are asking me to buy it and keep him in there! Where is the logic?! Wow, not sure how that happened. Too much is owed and I am not spending any more time trying to figure it out.

4. Another One Outside Town
[Source: Website]

This homeowner wants to sell a 3 bedroom, 2 bath, 1700-square-foot house outside of town.

Here are the numbers:

- Asking Price: Make an offer
- Amount Owed: $43,000
- Repairs: Very minor (unconfirmed)
- After Repaired Value: Unknown
- Max Offer: Unknown

The seller is facing a divorce and has no job. Things just aren't going well for him. I passed this one on to a wholesaler because it's just too far away and the numbers weren't looking beneficial.

--

This week I also got 6 leads I haven't mentioned. Most of these were unmotivated sellers or ones where they owed too much for the deal to be worthwhile.

Active deals

Historic House
Finally, I got another property under contract. This one should be a sweet deal. I will wholesale it and show the details once I've sold it. You can find the details of this deal in the Flipped Houses section at the end of the book. This one is the "Historic House."

This is a case where I did not think the seller would be very motivated as he already had contractors working on the house. I went by and looked it over and decided on a figure. Honestly, I was ready for him to get angry with my offer, but I made it anyway. He went on to inform me that he had hoped to get $X, which was just 10k more than what I was offering. I hadn't expected it and was very interested in the house at that price.

Just to make it seem more like a negotiation, I told him I would need to go and see it again to see if I can come up to his number. The next morning, I told him I would come up $5k at most, which was $5k below what he wanted. He told me he would have to think about it.

Here is a very important lesson that everyone should learn: when someone gives you a number that you like right from the get-go, do *not* immediately take it unless there is a lot of competition and you are at risk of losing it. People need to feel like they got the most they can possibly get. Sometimes, if they don't, they regret how the negotiations went and can get cold feet and back out of the deal. Even if it's just a couple thousand dollars or different terms, you should really negotiate.

He ended up calling me back that evening and was ready to deal. I met him first thing in the morning — with his attorney. The attorney proceeded to try and negotiate everything, including price, which of course had already been agreed upon. After he talked about all that he wanted, I told him I was not there to negotiate. The seller and I had already agreed on the deal.

After a brief spell, he came at me with, "You know, you are not the only person who buys houses," to which I responded, "And this is not the only house for sale. So, I guess we are in the same position, aren't we?"

After realizing that there would be no bullying, we had a good time. All went well.

Next steps

- Make lots of offers.
- Put out more bandit signs.
- Get more probate leads.
- Get another one under contract.

Week 10

Following Up Is Important

There are times when I frequently driving out to look at a single property — especially for a decent lead that's further out of town. What I decided to try doing is looking for some bank-owned or otherwise distressed listed properties near the house that I am going to see. I figure I might as well look at a couple others while I am out and about. I feel this is a better use of my time.

This week, I made six offers on listed properties, most of which were REO. I was targeting properties that have been on the market 45 days or more. I've had some counters, some rejections, and some I am still waiting on. I use my own lead management application to help keep track of the leads and follow up.

What it does is allow you to enter leads, notes and follow-up reminders, and helps you do some deal analysis. To me, the deal analysis part is the coolest, as you can play with the numbers quickly and easily. You can get access to it at flippilot.com

I also got some offers out and am following up. I'm sensing the next one is close. The number of leads we've been getting should be sufficient to meet my goals. I just have to keep this going and I'm sure to be able to buy the number of properties we want this year.

Lead Analysis

Lead source	Number of leads
Bandit signs	2
Yellow pages	4
Buying website	8
Drive for dollars	1
Probate	1
MLS	6
Wholesale	1
Referrals	1
Total	**24**

1. Divorcing and Need to Sell
[Source: Bandit Signs]

A homeowner wants to sell a 3 bedroom, 1.5 bath, 1500-square-foot house.

Here are the numbers:

- Asking Price: $70,000
- Amount Owed: $40,000
- Repairs: $20,000 (conservative and includes new AC)
- After Repaired Value: $90,000
- Max Offer: $38,000

The seller wants to sell due to divorce. The house looks good on Google Maps, but I went and looked at it and the front of the house was the only thing it had going for it. The house had several additions and a very amateurish garage apartment in the back. He had an inflated opinion of what the house was worth and was not on the same page as me regarding the repairs the house needed.

2. Tired Landlord
[Source: Drive for Dollars]

This homeowner wants to sell a 3 bedroom, 2 bath, 2000-square-foot house in a good neighborhood.

Here are the numbers:

- Asking Price: No idea
- Amount Owed: $65,000
- Repairs: Needs finishing (flooring, countertops, etc. unconfirmed)
- After Repaired Value: $125,000
- Max Offer: $80,000 minus repairs

The owner used to rent the house out, so when the tenants moved out, he started renovating it. He does not have the time nor the energy to finish the house and wanted to see what he could get for it. He was not motivated and I gave him a ballpark figure of somewhere in the $70's and he immediately said no. I will follow up.

3. Moving Out of Town [Def Leppard]
[Source: Bandit Signs]

A homeowner wants to sell a 4 bedroom, 3.5 bath, 2500-square-foot house.

Here are the numbers:

- Asking Price: $150,000
- Amount Owed: $0
- Repairs: $8,000
- After Repaired Value: $160,000
- Max Offer: $97,000

The seller wants to sell quickly so that she can move back to her hometown. She paid cash for the house a couple years ago and is negotiable. Even though she was asking close to retail, she seemed motivated, so I went to see the house. This is another tough one. I offered $95,000.

After following up, this did eventually become a deal for me, which you can follow in the coming weeks. Final numbers and further information can be found under "Def Leppard House" in the Flipping Houses section.

4. Ready to Be Done with It
[Source: Website]

This homeowner wants to sell a 4 bedroom, 3.5 bath, 2900-square-foot, newer house.

Here are the numbers:

- Asking Price: $300,000
- Amount Owed: $274,000
- Repairs: None (unconfirmed)
- After Repaired Value: $300,000
- Max Offer: $210,000 (70% of ARV) minus repairs

The seller is in the middle of a divorce and just wants to have everything over with. They don't want the house, but they just owe way too much. I used 70% of ARV because the house does not need anything based on the MLS pictures. That's another problem: they have it listed with a Realtor. Unless their agreement specifies that they can find a buyer themselves and not pay a commission, someone is going to have to pay the commission. Too much is owed, anyway. Next.

5. Large Inherited House
[Source: Website]

A homeowner wants to sell a 3 bedroom, 2.5 bath, 3000-square-foot house.

Here are the numbers:

- Asking Price: Make an offer
- Amount Owed: $0
- Repairs: Unknown

- After Repaired Value: $260,000
- Max Offer: $170,000 minus repairs

The seller inherited this house and is trying to avoid using a Realtor. The house is large and needs repairs. Hopefully, we can build a good rapport and help her to decide to sell quickly for cash. Sometimes it's hard with these higher dollar properties because the discount has to be so huge.

6. Inherited Property I Looked at in 2007
[Source: Yellow Pages]

A homeowner wants to sell a 3 bedroom, 3 bath, 1400-square-foot house.

Here are the numbers:

- Asking Price: Unknown
- Amount Owed: $45,000
- Repairs: $20,000
- After Repaired Value: $110,000
- Max Offer: $48,000

The caller found me in the Yellow Pages because he inherited the property. I was entering the information for the lead into my system and the record already existed. This happens from time to time and is always interesting. I'd looked at the property back in 2007 and had notes on what I had offered and what I had found out another investor had offered. I'll be making an offer.

--

In addition to these leads, I got 18 others this week, none of which panned out. Most simply owed too much or they were just not motivated enough to take what I could offer.

DANNY JOHNSON

Active deals

Hidden Iron House

We were not getting very many showings on the Hidden Iron House, so we reduced the price $5k. Some investors hold out to try and get the absolute top dollar and end up spending more in holding costs and problems. If there is no negative feedback about the house, dropping the price is one of the best ways to move it. I started this one a little higher to see if we could get it, so this quick price change is not hard to do.

Next steps

- Make lots of offers.
- Follow-ups.
- Prepare article on how to talk to sellers.

I want to leave you with a quote from a sign I saw yesterday as I was going to the airport to get some R&R: "Thinking will not overcome fear, but action will." This should be printed and posted on your computer or mirror in your bathroom. It sums up a lot of what keeps people on the sidelines.

Week 11

Got Another Deal

This week, I called on some follow-ups to see if anyone had changed their mind and one of them countered with me again. It's still not where I need to be, but it is much closer, so I'll be going back to the house to make another offer. It is much better to make offers in person as it is too easy for the other person to quickly say no on the phone. In person, people tend to consider things more and do not like to tell people no.

I've also re-submitted an offer on a bank-owned property that I found on MLS. The days on market are close to 60, so they'll be changing the price soon. I want to hit them right before the price change so that I'm not competing with several offers.

It has been 3 or 4 weeks since I mailed some of the drive for dollars prospects, so I prepared a mailing for this week. I printed out a batch of letters and signed each one and now I'm just waiting for our mailing person to stuff the envelopes and hand address them.

Leads Analyzed

Lead source	Number of leads
Bandit signs	4
Buying website	8
REO, MLS	3
Wholesale	2
Referrals	1
Total	**18**

1. Under Contract from Federal Tax Sale
[Source: Website]

An investor wants to sell their contract on a 3 bedroom, 2 bath, 1300-square-foot house in a so-so neighborhood.

Here are the numbers:

- Asking Price: $60,000
- Amount Owed: $58,000 (what they have it under contract for)
- Repairs: Says not much (unconfirmed)
- After Repaired Value: $80,000
- Max Offer: $50,000 minus repairs

The caller's business partner supposedly has this house under contract from a federal tax sale and could not get financing to buy it. I don't want it either for the price they have it for. This guy is just looking for the greater fool. Next.

2. Handicapped Son Requires Different Living Arrangements
[Source: Website]

A homeowner wants to sell their 3 bedroom, 3 bath, 2000-square-foot house.

Here are the numbers:

- Asking Price: Make an offer
- Amount Owed: Nothing
- Repairs: AC out and cosmetic (unconfirmed)
- After Repaired Value: $100,000
- Max Offer: $65,000 minus repairs

This seller has a handicapped son in a wheelchair and the house is two stories. She wants to get a new single-story house with wider doorways. The neighborhood has high days on market and only the sub-$60k-priced houses have sold over the last year. I passed this on as a bird-dog.

3. City Going to Demolish
[Source: Bandit Signs]

A homeowner wants to sell their 3 bedroom, 2 bath house in a bad area.

Here are the numbers:

- Asking Price: $25,000
- Amount Owed: $18,000
- Repairs: Everything
- After Repaired Value: Unknown
- Max Offer: Nothing

The seller needs to sell because the city is going to demolish the house. They informed the owner that if they find a buyer that intends to repair it immediately, they will stop the demolition. This would be good for me if the house was something I wanted. In the past, I've bought houses like this 'before' the demolition hearing and had to go to the hearing to inform them that I was buying and that I would repair it immediately. This one has already had its hearing and is set for demolition in a couple weeks. Even if it weren't being demolished, what they owe is actually a little much for a house in this area in the condition it's in. I passed this one on to an investor I know who buys in the area.

4. Divorce and Foreclosure
[Source: Referral]

This homeowner wants to sell their 3 bedroom, 3 bath, 3400-square-foot house in a good area.

Here are the numbers:

- Asking Price: $170,000
- Amount Owed: $159,000
- Repairs: Cosmetic (unconfirmed)
- After Repaired Value: Unknown
- Max Offer: Unknown

The seller is getting divorced and facing foreclosure, a double-whammy of sorts. I think what is owed is just a little too high, but did not research it fully. This is in an area where my father invests so I passed it on to him.

The problem with rural areas is that some of the houses were built by amateurs — people building their own house. Some are weird or built poorly, or both. This one was built by the seller's father. When asked what similar houses were selling for in the area, he responded with, "There is nothing else like this around here." Probably not a good thing.

5. Moving Out of State
[Source: Website]

A homeowner wants to sell their 4 bedroom, 3.5 bath, 3500-square-foot house in a great area.

Here are the numbers:

- Asking Price: $300,000
- Amount Owed: $165,000
- Repairs: $10,000 (cosmetic)
- After Repaired Value: $400,000
- Max Offer: $250,000

This seller is moving out of state for a great opportunity for her daughter. She has a great singing voice and has been offered a job teaching kids. They already have a place picked out that they don't want to lose either. Since they don't want to miss out on the opportunity, they were willing to sell at a deep discount. This price range in San Antonio can be hard to move. The days on market are usually a lot higher and holding costs can quickly get you in the red. The seller had already talked with a Realtor and got her opinion of what she could make and understands the trade-off. We'll see what happens.

--

In addition to the above leads, I got 13 others that just didn't have the numbers to work. Most owed too much while I just wasn't interested in the others.

Active deals

Historic House

Closing on the Historic House has been held up. There are two liens on the property and one should have paid off the other. The seller, so far, is not able to find any paperwork on the 2nd loan to show it actually did pay off the first. He says it did, but unfortunately, this is a problem that must be cleared up. The attorney for the seller says he is working on it. Hopefully, we can get this closed soon.

Week 12

This Is Why You Don't Give Up

I got very few leads this week. Until writing, I had only gotten six all week, but the last 24 hours brought in another six. I will have to keep pushing with the marketing I'm doing, but it's starting to get busy. I am still sending out letters and will attempt to drive for dollars again soon. Another priority is to find someone to go to the courthouse to research probates for me.

We now have three houses under contract, all awaiting closing, so I will be able to get more into the rehabbing and selling side of things soon

Lead Analysis

Lead source	Number of leads
Bandit signs	1
Yellow pages	1
Buying website	7
Drive for dollars	3
Total	**12**

1. Inherited and Needs Work
[Source: Yellow Pages]

This homeowner wants to sell a 4 bedroom, 2 bath, 2000-square-foot house in a good older neighborhood.

Here are the numbers:

- Asking Price: $100,000
- Amount Owed: $0
- Repairs: A lot — repairs not calculated yet
- After Repaired Value: Depends on rehab; $160k-225k
- Max Offer: $104k-135k minus repairs

This homeowner inherited the house and has no need for it. It needs a lot of repairs due to deferred maintenance and she does not want to deal with the hassle. I was unsure of her motivation because she seemed concerned about how we operate.

These types of sellers need a little extra explaining and talking to so that they are more comfortable with you. If you're subscribed to my blog (flippingjunkie.com) and received the *7 Crazy Real Estate Investing Stories*, you will recall the guy who thought we set up the attorney's office just for appearance to get him to sign over his house. We had to meet there to sign the contract as I wanted to lend more legitimacy to the whole thing, but he actually thought it was fake. You know, like in a movie where the guy goes back the next day and it is just a vacant warehouse.

The asking price on this house was reasonable, though, and so I went to see it this morning. I think the ARV would probably tend to be on the upper end of that scale because the house has a lot of character, but it also needs *a lot* of work!

2. Fixed Up to Sell
[Source: Drive for Dollars]

This homeowner wants to sell a 3 bedroom, 2 bath, 900-square-foot house in a decent neighborhood.

Here are the numbers:

- Asking Price: $75,000
- Amount Owed: $50,000

- Repairs: None (unconfirmed)
- After Repaired Value: $75,000
- Max Offer: $45,000

He fixed up the house with the intention to sell (sounds familiar). I'm not sure what it is with investors, but a lot of times they want to hide the fact that they are investors. I know when selling a house retail, people tend to be less apprehensive if they think they are buying from a homeowner that lived there — possibly because of the flipping houses shows, people think that we all 'slap lipstick on pigs.' This conversation didn't last long as we were wasting each other's time. Next.

3. Does Not Want to Rent
[Source: Website]

This homeowner wants to sell a 4 bedroom, 2.5 bath, 3100-square-foot house in a good neighborhood.

Here are the numbers:

- Asking Price: Make an offer
- Amount Owed: $135,000
- Repairs: Cosmetic (unconfirmed)
- After Repaired Value: $195,000
- Max Offer: $126,000 minus repairs

This seller moved out of town and rented the house. The tenants trashed it, so he moved back into the house and has been fixing it up again. He has since lost his job and has opportunities out of town and doesn't want to rent again for obvious reasons. This one just owes a little too much. The ARV is conservative because there are a lot of foreclosures to compete with in the area.

4. Major Surgery for Husband and Wife
[Source: Drive for Dollars]

These homeowners want to sell a 3 bedroom, 2 bath, 1300-square-foot house in a decent neighborhood.

Here are the numbers:

- Asking Price: Make an offer
- Amount Owed: $28,000
- Repairs: Cosmetic (unconfirmed)
- After Repaired Value: $90,000
- Max Offer: $58,000 minus repairs

This house was inherited and the owners are living there. They both have had surgery recently and cannot keep up with maintenance. They seemed really embarrassed about the state of the house and were hesitant to even schedule an appointment. I told them that I understand how hard it is to keep up with maintenance on a house even without medical problems and that I am only interested in the 'potential' the house has and don't care what shape it is currently in. They seemed more relaxed immediately.

--

The 8 other leads from this week were nothing special. Most owe too much, although I was able to pass two on to other investors.

Active deals

Def Leppard House
We finally got another house under contract! Our marketing is starting to bring steady deals now as new leads come in and I follow up on old ones. This was one I had made an offer on a couple of weeks ago. Honestly, I didn't think she would change her mind, but she did.

This house would have sold for $180k two years ago. It still might get $170k and I will try to get that at first. I had offered $95k and she was not at all happy with it. Several days later, I called and asked if she had thought about it. She asked if I could pay $120k and I told her the most I could do was $100k. Several days later she called and mentioned that another investor had offered her $105k and wanted to know if I could do $110k. I knew I couldn't but scheduled with her to take my wife by to see it.

The reason I didn't just tell her that $100k was the most I could do over the phone was that it would have been too easy for her to just say no and call the other investor back. I wanted more time in the deal and to discuss it face-to-face.

My wife and I went over to the house and we sat and talked a little while and then told her that I just could not pay more than $100k. She asked if I could do the $105k the other investor had offered and I quickly told her that I just couldn't. At $100k, I knew I could close it and she could consider it a done deal. I told her we could close before that weekend and allow her to stay in the house 5 days after closing if we withheld $5,000 until she vacated ($100/day penalty for every day over — this is very important). She accepted.

She told us that she went with us because she trusted us and liked us. I always like to hear that because I know the way I treat sellers makes all the difference in the world. This proves that you can pay less than another investor and still get the deal if you're nice about it.

Historic House
We are still awaiting Chase to send a release of lien on the property. The seller has informed me that he sent everything they asked for and we are just waiting for them.

Next steps
- Look for probate gatherer or do it myself.
- Follow-up calls.
- Find time to sign up for Accurint again and find owners of the worst drive for dollars properties.
- Close on the property we got under contract this week.

Week 13

Who Ya Gonna Call?

This week, we got close to putting another house under contract. I went and looked at the first lead for this week (see below). The seller got divorced several years ago and the house is now vacant. The ex is remarrying and wants to have the house out of her name, so she wants it sold.

The property was in good shape; it just needed cosmetic repairs for the most part. The master bathroom could use another vanity.

After walking through the house, it got really interesting. The seller informed me that the house is haunted. He had seen a young blonde girl that looked like she was straight out of *Little House on the Prairie* on two occasions. The first was during a party they were having and he was walking to the kitchen to get a drink and happened to look up the stairs and saw her standing there looking at him and she smiled really big. The other time, he was lying in bed and watching TV and she walked in and stood between the bed and the TV and just looked at him for a couple seconds and then turned and walked out of the room. I feel weird just typing this.

He then told me that he had a plumber working on the master bath one day and he and his wife had left the house. The plumber called shortly afterward and asked him if they had left someone at the house with him. The seller then told him not to worry about it, that it was just a ghost. The plumber then laughed awkwardly and hung up. When they got home, the plumber had all his tools in his truck and was leaving with the job unfinished. He never did come back.

Sort of creepy. Out of the 18 years, he only saw her twice and he said it has been a while.

Anyway, the numbers looked pretty good but I needed to offer just above what they owed. I really didn't think he would at all be interested in this. Well, maybe he would have been after the story he just told me. I offered $50k which was my maximum. After rechecking the comparable sales, I'm sure I can make it work at the $54k he wants, but he would have to pay title policy and his part of the closing costs.

Apart from that lead, I set up another drive for dollars mailing as another batch had come due. I printed and signed each one and my daughters are working on hand addressing these. (I bribed them with a little money and a trip to Orange Leaf).

I also called Accurint for pricing information this week. It seems they've gone up. It used to be about $150/mo and now they are at $300/mo. This might be a little much. I'd be okay with it if I could pay for a month at a time, but they want a year-long commitment.

This week, I had so few leads I actually had to check on the website to make sure it's still up and running. It looks fine, so I guess this is just a slow week.

Lead Analysis

Lead source	Number of leads
Yellow pages	1
Buying website	3
Drive for dollars	1
Total	**5**

1. Divorce Situation
[Source: Website]

A homeowner wants to sell a 3 bedroom, 2.5 bath, 1700-square-foot house in a decent neighborhood.

Here are the numbers:

- Asking Price: Make an offer
- Amount Owed: $48,000
- Repairs: None (unconfirmed)
- After Repaired Value: $89,000
- Max Offer: $57,000 minus repairs

This seller is divorcing and moving in with his disabled parents to help them out. I thought he wasn't very motivated as he was refusing to tell me how much is owed. In this case, I didn't want to waste time so I told him a ballpark figure would be in the $50's depending on repairs. He was actually willing to consider it and was going to talk to the ex. I followed up the next day and he told me to come and look at it and we could talk about it, so I did. I was working on buying this one, but it didn't end up happening.

2. Piece of Junk on Corner Lot
[Source: Drive for Dollars]

A homeowner wants to sell a 2 bedroom, 1 bathroom, 800-square-foot house.

Here are the numbers:

- Asking Price: $35,000
- Amount Owed: $0
- Repairs: $20,000 (unconfirmed)
- After Repaired Value: $60,000
- Max Offer: $30,000 minus repairs

This seller is an older investor who has been buying and selling for 40 years! She really talked up a big game about how much potential the house has. I actually went and looked at this house over a year ago and it is a real dump. The corner lot is right on a busy road in a rental neighborhood. She says she turned down an offer for $25k already and I know I will be below that, so I am not going to waste my time. I did ask what her buying criteria were in case I come across something she might be interested in — didn't want to let this call be a complete waste.

--

This week I had three other leads, two of which I passed on to others. The other was not motivated.

Active deals

Def Leppard House
We closed on this deal from last week and are just waiting for the seller to move out before we begin work. Since I need to come up with names for these houses so I don't get them all confused, this house will be called the "Def Leppard House" because the seller was a big fan. More details about this deal will come up in the next few weeks, and you can find final numbers and project details in the Flipped Houses section at the end of the book.

Historic House
We are *still* awaiting Chase to send a release of lien on this property. We are checking with them every 2-3 days to make sure someone is pushing to get this thing done. Geez, I hate waiting.

Hidden Iron House
We accepted an offer on the Hidden Iron House yesterday. Final numbers and rehab details are in the Flipped Houses section.

Next steps
- Look for probate gatherer or do it myself.
- Follow-ups.
- Have fun with some time off.

Week 14

Thank You!

One day this week, I had two appointments in the morning. The first one, nobody showed up! I had gotten up early to be there and I was pretty tired from being at Six Flags all day the day before. When I called the seller and asked if she planned on meeting me, she said she couldn't make it and had called her brother to see if he would show up but he wasn't available. For whatever reason, she did not feel it necessary to call me! What is wrong with people?

While talking to her, I was trying my best to not say something to that effect and keep my cool. She then informed me of how badly they needed to sell it and asked if I could give them an idea based on the exterior. With this, I had to assume most everything inside would have to be fixed or replaced and offered $15k.

They are likely doing this to other investors as well and the ones that get angry and do not try to keep a good rapport will lose out on the deal if it becomes one, so it's important to not complain to the seller about things they do.

The second appointment was for a seller that had called me back in January. I had gone by to see his house and made him an offer then. He finally called me back (after 6 months) and said he wants to go ahead and sell it. We agreed to meet at the house at 11:00 today and sign the contract.

I got to the house and sat down with him to go over the contract and he was really nervous. Small conversation and chit chat did not seem to help any. He then informed me that he hadn't talked with his ex about the deal. What? You mean you did not talk with her first, during that whole 6 months?! So now I'm wondering about the whole thing. How hard should I push? Not very. I left the contract with him and told him I really need to know something by tomorrow because I have other houses to see and need to know if my money might be tied up. I did end up making a deal with this one. I'm calling it the Frustration House, and more details will follow in the coming weeks. You can also find full details of the deal in the Flipped Houses section.

I was also at the courthouse last week and gathered some leads for another probate mailing.

Overall, my leads increased from the low last week. Last Friday, one slipped through my hands as I waited two hours too late to call and the people I was in touch with informed the decision maker of the wrong number. Another investor ended up with it. I'm getting really close on some this week and feel like we should have a couple more under contract soon.

Lead Analysis

Lead source	Number of leads
Bandit signs	5
Buying website	8
Drive for dollars	2
Total	**15**

1. Unrealistic. Wants more than the crap house is worth.
[Source: Website]

This homeowner wants to sell a 2 bedroom, 1 bath, 800-square-foot house in a bad neighborhood.

Here are the numbers:

- Asking Price: Make an offer
- Amount Owed: $0

- Repairs: $10k (based on conversation — unconfirmed)
- After Repaired Value: $55,000
- Max Offer: $30,000 minus repairs

The seller inherited the house from his dad and the dad had a crew working to fix it up. The son has the job of making sure the work is done right but is having a tough time. Tough time with contractors, imagine that.

There is an inherent clash between investors and contractors whereby investors want the best work at the cheapest possible cost and contractors wants the work done to a decent standard for the highest possible cost, which is understandable. Each side is right and this can obviously lead to a lot of problems. It's always a balancing act keeping everyone happy and chugging along (hopefully not chugging beer all day, as has happened before with a foundation crew — not good!).

The seller mainly didn't want to deal with the hassles of the property and I think he did not really care for the area. I passed this one on to a wholesaler friend of mine because the guy did not seem terribly motivated.

2. Moving Out of State
[Source: Yellow Pages]

A homeowner wants to sell a 2 bedroom, 1 bath, 1200-square-foot house in a so-so neighborhood.

Here are the numbers:

- Asking Price: $74,000
- Amount Owed: $39,000
- Repairs: $15,000 (guesstimate based on conversation — unconfirmed)
- After Repaired Value: $85,000
- Max Offer: $55,000 minus repairs

The seller is moving out of state and needs to sell this house. She has it listed with a Realtor, but the listing is going to expire soon. The house was put under contract, but the buyer backed out when the inspection came back with a mention that the foundation needs work. The seller got an estimate for a couple grand for the foundation but does not want to spend the money on the house. This one was built in 1920 and does not have central air conditioning. The repairs consist of fixing the foundation and associated damage from that and adding central air and some updating. I told her I would need to be in the 40's and she was not at all interested.

3. Fire Damaged and Vacant for 3 Years
[Source: Drive for Dollars]

This homeowner wants to sell a 3 bedroom, 2 bath, 2000-square-foot house in a good neighborhood.

Here are the numbers:

- Asking Price: Make an offer
- Amount Owed: Unknown (still waiting to find out)
- Repairs: Quite a bit (unconfirmed)
- After Repaired Value: $135,000
- Max Offer: $85,000 minus repairs

This is a super motivated seller. The mother-in-law passed away and the house has fire damage. The city also has a case against the house for not keeping it clean and secure. I have to go by and try to get in, as the sellers live out of town. This one might take a little while to work. More on this story next week.

4. Moving and Want to Buy Another House
[Source: Yellow Pages]

A homeowner wants to sell a 3 bedroom, 2.5 bath, 1800-square-foot house in a good neighborhood.

Here are the numbers:

- Asking Price: Make an offer
- Amount Owed: $25,000

- Repairs: $12,000
- After Repaired Value: $100,000
- Max Offer: $48,000

This one is down the street from the ghost house from last week. The seller wants to buy another house, but needs to sell this one first and does not want to wait. She knows the market is very slow right now and just wants to get going. There is equity and some motivation, so I went to see the house and make an offer.

One of the neighbors is super junky and will definitely make it hard to sell this house. Because of this, I decided to offer even less than normal because I would want to wholesale this one to avoid sitting on the house forever — not to mention the possibility of the house getting vandalized while vacant.

I ended up offering $40k and made a point to let them know that the reason is the neighbor. They then confirmed that the neighbors don't work and party all the time. Nice. I told her to contact code compliance.

5. Parents Are Going to Assisted Living
[Source: Website]

The homeowner wants to sell a 2 bedroom, 1 bath, 1200-square-foot house in a so-so neighborhood.

Here are the numbers:

- Asking Price: Make an offer
- Amount Owed: $0
- Repairs: Quite a bit (unconfirmed)
- After Repaired Value: $65,000
- Max Offer: $35,000 minus repairs

This is the caller's parents' house and they are going into assisted living and need to sell the house. This house was built in 1926 and does not have central air. I want to be able to buy this cheap enough to either wholesale or sell with owner financing. This is the one I mentioned at the beginning about no one showing up to meet me. We didn't end up making a deal on this one.

6. Moving and Needs to Sell
[Source: Website]

This homeowner wants to sell a 3 bedroom, 2 bath, 1300-square-foot house in a not-so-good neighborhood.

Here are the numbers:

- Asking Price: Make an offer
- Amount Owed: $0
- Repairs: Quite a bit (leveling, cosmetic — unconfirmed)
- After Repaired Value: $70,000
- Max Offer: $40,000 minus repairs

This seller simply wants to move and not deal with the hassles of selling a house in this market. The house needs a lot of repairs and is in an area that is mostly rentals and owner-financed houses. I went to meet the seller at the house and a strange guy was waiting out front. When I got out of my car and introduced myself, he started acting funny and asking what this was all about. He must have taken a bath in cheap cologne, too, because I could barely breathe and could still smell it on my hand hours after shaking his hand.

He informed me that the house is his son's and he is not selling it. It was obvious the dad was not interested and I was not going to waste my time. The mom was the one who had called me, so I called her. She did not pick up, but did call back two minutes later with a blocked phone number. She mentioned the house is the son's and that the dad lives there and needs to move because the son wants to move to Louisiana. When asked, she said the dad was on the title and when I mentioned that the deal could not be done without his signature, she changed the story and said he wasn't. I told her to get it all straightened out and call me when I could actually see the house.

I don't know that I would go back anyway as she didn't bother to tell me she was going to be a no-show at the house this morning. Some people! I could not imagine making an appointment and then not showing or at least calling and apologizing.

--

The 9 other leads this week didn't get anywhere. One was bird-dogged and I couldn't make it work with the others. A frustrating week with some of these owners.

Active deals

Def Leppard House

The Def Leppard House is now being rehabbed. The seller moved out over the weekend and I was able to go in with my contractor on Tuesday to go over the scope of work. We agreed on a price today and my contractor is starting work tomorrow.

My guy is doing the repairs for $3,400 and I have a carpet cleaner going by to give me an estimate to let me know whether he thinks he can make the carpet look like new. If we can clean them, instead of replacing them, we'll save a lot of money. I'm sure there will be other miscellaneous items that pop up as well.

You can find more information about this deal, including numbers, timeline and scope of work in the Flipped Houses section at the end of the book.

Historic House

Last Friday, the seller for this house that we have been trying to close called me and was pretty upset. He mentioned that his attorney had found the release of lien we had been trying to get from Chase. It was apparently already recorded at the courthouse. I was floored as well and was wondering why the title company did not find it. It turns out that the recorded document was not associated with the house for some reason.

The seller had a right to be angry as he had spent no less than 15 hours on the phone trying to get the release. Well, now we are having trouble with Chase getting the payoff, but that should not be too bad. Hopefully, we'll have this thing closed by tomorrow or early next week.

Hidden Iron House
The inspection for the Hidden Iron House was completed and went well. Mainly minor things like the kitchen faucet leak and some damaged shingles were mentioned. These things will be fixed within the next couple days and we will continue to be on track for our scheduled closing date and our payday. The numbers should look pretty good on this one and I will share those in the Flipped Houses section.

Next steps

- Get more probate leads.
- Call follow-ups (you can setup automatic follow-up reminders using my house flipping software, available at flippilot.com).
- Check on Def Leppard rehab.
- Fix items from Hidden Iron House inspection.

Week 15

The Death House

This week, I went to look at a house lead from last week (#3) where there was fire damage. The house has been vacant for more than two years. The seller lives out of town and doesn't visit the house often. Code compliance is getting on them about the house — the yard is overgrown and there is a lot of trash. It looks like it has been ransacked.

The seller informed me that his mother-in-law passed away in the house due to smoke inhalation. I was expecting major fire damage to this house and was surprised to not see any from the exterior. We went in through the back door which was unlocked. After practically wading through the trash and around the large mattresses on the living room floor, we entered the kitchen.

There were signs of a grease fire that burned the upper cabinets and had very minor smoke damage above. We could not figure out how someone could have died from this fire. The neighbor was outside and we went to see what they knew. It seems that the mother-in-law had emphysema and inhaled too much smoke while putting out the fire. Sad. She also informed us that her nephew had passed away from a drug overdose several months prior to the fire. I don't know if that occurred in this house or not.

There was a notice posted from a bank on the window and now I need to find out if they've already lost the house and didn't even know. The seller did mention that he thought there was a lien on the house. I'm sure he wasn't making payments if he didn't know about this. Now, it's been vacant for several years, so I am confident that the bank probably did take the house already. It's strange that the county tax rolls still show the mother-in-law as the owner, though.

I'm going to make contact with the seller again tomorrow and see if we can't get this all figured out. I'll definitely need to buy this one super cheap — wholesale style.

Overall, leads increased again this week from the low two weeks ago. I'll be pushing the historic wholesale big time over the next week to other investors. If I don't get any solid bites quickly, I will attempt to sell to someone looking to live in it and fix it up.

I called follow-ups from previous weeks, but nothing has changed yet. I also went down to the courthouse last week and gathered some leads for another probate mailing. I sent out the first batch for envelope addressing and stuffing and should be able to mail those out early next week.

Lead Analysis

Lead source	Number of leads
Bandit signs	1
Yellow pages	3
Buying website	14
Drive for dollars	1
Wholesale	1
FSBO	1
Total	**21**

1. Inherited Large, Very Outdated House
[Source: Website]

The homeowner wants to sell a 5 bedroom, 4.5 bath, 4500-square-foot house in a good neighborhood.

Here are the numbers:

- Asking Price: Make an offer
- Amount Owed: Nothing
- Repairs: $80,000 (at least)

- After Repaired Value: $420,000
- Max Offer: $196,000

I knew what the house would be like as soon as they told me the size and the neighborhood. This neighborhood is full of these houses that were built in the 60's and they all still have the same style. It's like some weird time warp — nobody ever updates their houses. These things are huge, too, so it will cost a small fortune. The sellers all tend to have super inflated ideas of their value because the houses seem livable and clean. But, man are they outdated. Have you ever been to Graceland? If so, you've been to one of these houses.

They inherited the house and have been trying to sell it through a Realtor. The Realtor has it priced as if it were completely updated and only has one picture in the MLS. I made them an offer of $195k and they are not interested. I've passed this on to another investor that said he would pay more and hopefully they can strike up a deal so I can get a referral fee.

2. Tagged and Boarded Up
[Source: FSBO]

This homeowner wants to sell a 3 bedroom, 1 bath, 1000-square-foot townhouse in a so-so neighborhood.

Here are the numbers:

- Asking Price: $45,000
- Amount Owed: Unknown
- Repairs: Unknown
- After Repaired Value: $75,000
- Max Offer: $45,000 minus repairs

I saw this one while driving over to look at another lead. The house is boarded up and tagged with graffiti. There was a For Sale by Owner sign in the front yard, so I called the seller. It turns out I had received a call about this house a year ago, which I found when entering the information for the lead into my lead manager. He still wants a little much for this property, but is close enough for another investor I know, so I passed the lead on to him.

3. Tenant For 30 Years
[Source: Drive for Dollars]

The homeowner wants to sell a 3 bedroom, 2 bath, 1000-square-foot townhouse in a so-so neighborhood.

Here are the numbers:

- Asking Price: Make an offer
- Amount Owed: Unknown
- Repairs: Unknown
- After Repaired Value: $70,000
- Max Offer: $40,000 minus repairs

This seller called and mentioned that she has had the same tenant in the house for 30 years. She wants to sell, but doesn't have the heart to kick the tenant out. There are a lot of people who worry about this and there are also a lot of landlords who are afraid of their tenants, though this is not the case here. I am working up a ballpark figure to see if she wants to move forward. Obviously, a big selling point will be that she will not have to do anything with the tenant.

After researching for a minute, it turns out this is the junky house next to a wholesale deal I looked at a couple of weeks ago. This house needs *a lot* of repairs and so she really needs to be excited about the ballpark for me to want to go and look because I know I will need to come off of that number by quite a bit to cover the repair costs. When I called, she said she's not interested. Glad I didn't waste any more time. Next.

--

The 18 other leads from the week were a mix of out of area properties I was able to pass on to other investors and sellers who I just couldn't make a deal with.

Active deals

Def Leppard House
The rehab on the Def Leppard House is being wrapped up and should be finished next week.

Historic House
We *finally* closed on the historic house that I intend to wholesale. I had decided to wait until after closing to push out this deal because the attorney for the seller lives across the street and I did not want any problems with the deal. Find further information about this deal in the Flipped Houses section.

Hidden Iron House
The inspection for the Hidden Iron House was completed and some small repairs were required. Not bad. The appraisal is complete and all repairs should be done any day now — we're just waiting on the survey and closing.

Next steps

- Get more probate leads.
- Call follow-ups.
- Finish and start staging Def Leppard rehab.
- Push Historic House wholesale.

Week 16

Frustration House Under Contract

This week was slow, but it was the Fourth of July weekend. I'm sure next week will show a decent increase in leads again. I have probate letters going out and will try to put out bandit signs. We also stuffed probate letters into envelopes and hand addressed them. Now, I just need to stick them in the mail. I hesitate to put too many letters in the mail all at one time because part of me feels there is temptation for the mailman to think it is junk and throw some away. I don't know where that fear came from, but it's there.

One of the houses I was going to buy but could not get them quite low enough is going under contract soon with an investor I worked out a deal with. I should make $3k on that one for bird-dogging and negotiating with the seller.

Lead Analysis

Lead source	Number of leads
Wholesale	2
Buying website	7
Total	9

1. Moving Out of State
[Source: Website]

A homeowner wants to sell a 3 bedroom, 1 bath, 800-square-foot house in a bad neighborhood.

Here are the numbers:

- Asking Price: $40,000
- Amount Owed: $0
- Repairs: Not much (unconfirmed)
- After Repaired Value: $45,000
- Max Offer: $20,000 minus repairs

This seller wants to move out of state. This neighborhood is pretty rough and really just good for rental or owner financing. I'm sure there are other investors that will pay more than me for this one, so I passed it on in hopes of getting a bird-dog fee. Next.

2. Horrible Property Management
[Source: Website]

The homeowner wants to sell this 3 bedroom, 2.5 bath, 1600-square-foot house in a decent neighborhood.

Here are the numbers:

- Asking Price: Make an offer
- Amount Owed: $90,000
- Repairs: Mostly cosmetic (unconfirmed)
- After Repaired Value: $100,000
- Max Offer: $65,000 minus repairs

This seller is in the military and has been transferred. She hired a local property management company and they did what most will do and stuck bad tenants in the house. Several times, she's had to evict people and the house has been trashed every single time. She is sick and tired of taking leave to come back and dump tons of money into the house so that the next tenants can tear it up all over again. It just blows my mind how people can have no respect for other people's property — this is also why I don't care for rentals. They look awesome on paper, but the reality of bad tenants and headaches can quickly turn you sour.

This one owes too much for anything to really be done. She is not behind on payments. I'll just have to move on to the next one.

--

The other 7 leads from this week were mostly ones that owed too much or were in horrible neighborhoods. Moving on.

Active deals

Def Leppard House
The rehab on the Def Leppard House is being wrapped up and should be finished next week. It's taking a little while longer as we've had problems with the Homeowner's Association. My contractor painted the front door a nice deep red to make it stand out and the hall monitor (what I call the guy from the HOA) got his panties all in a bunch. It appears that the color needed to be approved before we could paint it. You should have seen it before — it was so ugly that I am now assuming the previous owner was trying to get back at the HOA!

I've put in a call in to the hall monitor and he has not returned it. If he doesn't today, I am giving the go-ahead to give it a second coat and put on the new hardware. I can't wait around for this guy to come by and bless everything. Gotta love flipping houses.

Historic House
I am very excited to say that a couple days after closing, I was able to sell the historic house to the first person I called. That was quick. Maybe I should just wholesale from now on... Nah, there's too much to be made with rehabs.

Hidden Iron House
I should have known things were going too smoothly for the Hidden Iron House closing. We ran into a problem with the FHA loan the buyer is getting. Being that we have not owned the house for more than 90 days, they needed to make sure we were not making more than 20% profit. This drives me freaking nuts.

107

Of course, we are making more than that and so I'll have to work on getting the contract rewritten to show that it was contracted after 91 days and get a second appraisal to make sure we are not ripping anybody off. This is just plain ridiculous — just more hoops to jump through. We've had this happen many times in the past and it has never killed a deal, so we are not really worried about it.

Frustration House
This is the house from Week 14 where the guy hadn't talked to his ex about the deal. Well, after questions from him every couple of days (even calling one evening at 8:30), he finally called to see when I could come by to get the contract. This time, I made sure that his wife had already signed before heading over.

The visit was pleasant and all went well and I receipted the contract a few days later. Then, the dreaded call came this afternoon when he told me he wanted to net more money. I told him it was pointless to talk about net as we weren't sure of what it would be exactly until the numbers were worked out. Trust me, I tried to be as polite as possible and I hope the true level of aggravation and frustration I was feeling didn't show through.

This sort of situation needs to be nipped in the bud as soon as it shows up. If I were to give in and give him more concessions after we've signed the contract, he would just keep asking for more. I am keeping my word and closing the deal at the agreed upon terms and I expect him to do the same. Period.

Next steps
- Call follow-ups.
- Mail letters.
- Get the Def Leppard House cleaned and start staging.
- Try to get bandit signs out.
- Line up financing for the Frustration House.

Week 17

Guess I'm Chewy

This week, I got chewed out again from a letter. You really do need to develop somewhat of a thick skin if you are going into flipping houses or any sort of business. Mostly, I just need it for dealing with contractors and people I send letters to. It just blows my mind how many people get so angry about someone sending them a letter asking them if they would like to sell their house. Do like most normal people and just throw the thing away if you're not interested.

This particular caller did not appreciate that I had sent him a letter and wondered why I targeted him and how I got his information. I politely explained that I got his information from the county tax office. He asked why I had sent the letter to him when he did not have a sign out front. I mistakenly told him that I must have noticed his house while driving the area and it looked like it needed some repairs. Of course, he did not like this very much. Oops. Oh well, we can't make everybody happy, can we?

I mailed probate letters last Friday and only received a couple calls and these were just wanting me to remove them from the mailing list. One was none too polite about it. She had left a message and I suppose she was more comfortable leaving a message to tell me what she thought of me and my business. She then went on to tear apart my letter and to tell me how much of a grammatical disaster it was. Another happy customer.

I also had 40 bandit signs put out over the weekend. I don't know if they've stayed up as I haven't received very many calls — and it's already time for me to order more.

The leads did pick up again this week. Monday was spent frantically handling most of these leads as they all seemed to come in that morning. It was crazy. The rest of the week was a little more relaxed and I even got to fly a Piper Cub on Monday afternoon, which was awesome.

I bird-dogged a lot of leads this week and am sure to make some money from those. Nothing seemed good enough for me to want to take down myself. Something should come along soon, though.

Lead Analysis

Lead source	Number of leads
Bandit signs	1
Yellow pages	4
Buying website	15
Drive for dollars	1
Total	21

1. We Protested The #$%! Out of the Taxes
[Source: Website]

This homeowner wants to sell a 2 bedroom, 1 bath, 900-square-foot house in a not-so-good neighborhood.

Here are the numbers:

- Asking Price: $60,000
- Amount Owed: $45,000
- Repairs: Minor (unconfirmed)
- After Repaired Value: $65,000
- Max Offer: $40,000 minus repairs

This seller says they completely remodeled the house but want to move. He went on to inform me that the neighbors all got together and protested the $#%@ out of the taxes. Too funny. Looking at the county tax appraisal

110

district website, however, doesn't show much in the way of a decrease over the last 5 years. There is one but not more than $3-5k.

In our last primary residence, a historic house, the city tried to up the taxes almost 300% in one year. The house did go from looking like the Paper Street house in *Fight Club* to a like-new condition. I'm glad those days of fighting so hard to keep the tax value down are over. Back to this one. He owes a little too much for my liking and will pass this lead on as a bird-dog.

2. Does Not Want to Make Another Payment
[Source: Website]

The homeowner wants to sell a 2 bedroom, 1 bath, 900-square-foot house in a decent neighborhood.

Here are the numbers:

- Asking Price: $52,000
- Amount Owed: $43,000
- Repairs: Some (unconfirmed)
- After Repaired Value: $80,000
- Max Offer: Can't offer

The seller called from a letter we sent and mentioned that another investor had made an offer and she wanted to get a second one. I went through all of my typical questions and talked about everything the house had.

Then, I asked about the other investor's offer. She promptly told me what his offer was and I was immediately thinking that it was a good, high offer and I likely could not beat it. I asked if he was wanting to sign a contract to which she replied that she did sign something. She then read the top of the "thing" she signed and it was a standard contract. She didn't even know she was under contract to sell the house.

Now, I don't know if the investor is to blame for not explaining things clearly or if she was just not all there. Either way, I had to inform her that she already had the house sold and it was just a matter of it closing. Next.

DANNY JOHNSON

3. Twelve Months Behind
[Source: Website]

A homeowner wants to sell a 3 bedroom, 2.5 bath, 2800-square-foot house in a decent neighborhood.

Here are the numbers:

- Asking Price: $163,000
- Amount Owed: $163,000 taxes
- Repairs: Minor (unconfirmed)
- After Repaired Value: $125,000
- Max Offer: $80,000 minus repairs

This seller needs to sell this house because he is behind on payments *by a year*. This house is from a previous marriage and he has since moved on. This is an area that has been hit hard with price drops caused by competition with foreclosures, so it would be a perfect candidate for a short sale.

4. I Thought It Would Be an Expensive House
[Source: Yellow Pages]

The homeowner wants to sell a 2 bedroom, 1 bath, 900-square-foot house in a bad neighborhood.

Here are the numbers:

- Asking Price: $55,000
- Amount Owed: $0
- Repairs: Minor (unconfirmed)
- After Repaired Value: $50,000
- Max Offer: $25,000 minus repairs

This call was interesting. The seller had an English accent and she wanted to describe every single thing about the house. I started getting anxious as I knew she just wasn't that motivated as she went on and on about how the house was in a historic district. At this point, I was figuring this was a

$300k+ house, which is a lot for San Antonio. After her lengthy description, we got down to details. It turns out this house is in the middle of the worst area of San Antonio. It really shocked me.

This one ended with me informing her that we typically buy in the teens in the area, to which she was none too happy. Sorry. Next.

5. Mom Wanted Them to Sell
[Source: Website]

The homeowner wants to sell a 5 bedroom, 2 bath, 2000-square-foot house in a bad neighborhood.

Here are the numbers:

- Asking Price: $30,000
- Amount Owed: $11,000
- Repairs: A lot (unconfirmed)
- After Repaired Value: $65,000
- Max Offer: Not for me

The seller inherited the house and her mother wanted them to sell it after she passed. This area is not one that I buy in, but I passed the lead on as they were already asking a somewhat reasonable price.

I found out from the investor I sent this lead to that there was a murder there very recently. He says that the husband killed his wife in the shed in the back of the property. Sad. He got it under contract for a good price, of course, and says it will take a while to close because of probate issues. Always interesting things happening in this business...

7. Tire-Kicker from Third Letter
[Source: Drive for Dollars]

This homeowner wants to sell a 3 bedroom, 2 bath, 1400-square-foot house in a good neighborhood.

Here are the numbers:

- Asking Price: Make an offer
- Amount Owed: Wouldn't say
- Repairs: Minor (unconfirmed)
- After Repaired Value: $100,000
- Max Offer: $65,000 minus repairs

This seller finally called after receiving three letters from me. She mentioned they were considering selling and wanted to know how much I would offer before they listed with a Realtor. I made them a ballpark estimate in the 60's. No go, so far. I have always gone back and forth on whether to keep sending a series of letters and postcards after the first couple. It seems the motivated ones call mostly from the first letter. This time I am going to continue to send them as I feel that maybe my message will be "burned" into their mind a little more and there is more of a chance they will keep at least one of the letters.

--

The 16 other leads from this week were a mix of the same—some just owed too much, others were simply delusional about what their home is worth or they were just in a terrible area. I was able to pass a few on to other investors.

Active deals

Def Leppard House
While rehabbing the Def Leppard House, I decided to try to just have the carpet cleaned instead of replacing it with new. This is a 2500 square foot house and the carpet was filthy. My carpet cleaning guy told me he could get it clean and it would only cost $175. The risk versus reward was good enough to go ahead and try.

After the carpet was cleaned, I went by to check out the job. The carpet was much cleaner but still had a lot of small stains everywhere. This would have been acceptable for a rental but not for a house that will retail around $170,000 (which is above the median in San Antonio). At least I didn't pay much. I then had to make a call to my carpet guy and he agreed to remove the old carpet and install new for $1,900. Great price.

This all caused a bit of a delay, but we are getting it all wrapped up. The cleaning crew will be in on Friday and my wife went to purchase staging furniture and other items. We are just starting to stage the houses we sell and my wife and our Realtor have done an incredible job picking out spectacular pieces. This will be the second house flip she's staged, so she wrote a piece about what she's learned, which you can get at http://www.flippingjunkie.com/2011/staging-a-house-flip-lesson-learned.

My wife kicks butt, doesn't she?

Historic House
The historic house that we are wholesaling is supposed to close on the sell side tomorrow.

Hidden Iron House
We are *still* working on the closing for this house. Not much to say, although we have things ironed out and are just waiting to close.

Frustration House
The seller called Friday evening while we were having dinner. The phone went to voicemail because I don't answer the phone at the dinner table, but that didn't stop me from worrying about what the message was going to be. My immediate thought was that he was going to tell me the deal was off. As soon as we were finished with dinner, I checked my messages. He had called to apologize for how he acted the other day when he told me he wanted more money after we had already signed the contract. I guess my handling of it worked and I was successful in nipping that in the bud. We are set to close next week.

Next steps
- Prepare letters for mailing.
- Put Def Leppard House on the market.
- Get some more probate leads.
- Close on the Frustration House.

Week 18

The $50,000 Wholesale

This week, I mailed out about 75 probate letters and have not received any calls yet. It's too early to really tell, but I might need to split test my letters and try to find a better performing one.

We're still working on the Hidden Iron House closing as well.

Overall, leads have picked up again this week. I've slowed down a little on marketing and will pick that back up again soon after our upcoming vacation.

If you're interested in some of our favorite businesses and house flipping books, we've set up a Resources page on the website. We'll keep updating it as time permits, and you can access it at http://www.flippingjunkie.com/house-flipping-resources

Lead Analysis

Lead source	Number of leads
Bandit signs	5
Yellow pages	1
Buying website	8
Referrals	2
Total	16

1. Strange Seller
[Source: Website]

The homeowner wants to sell a 3 bedroom, 2 bath, 2000-square-foot house in a good neighborhood.

Here are the numbers:

- Asking Price: Make an offer
- Amount Owed: $63,000
- Repairs: Unknown (unconfirmed)
- After Repaired Value: $105,000
- Max Offer: $68,000 minus repairs

The seller submitted the form on my website, but when I tried to call her to ask some more questions and gauge her motivation, she sounded strange and asked if I could call back at noon. She didn't pick up again and I tried several times.

When I finally got back in touch, I found out that they want to move back to Vegas. I mentioned that I would need to buy around what she owed and she seemed to be taken aback. The problem is the competition with foreclosures in the area, which has brought the value down. She was under the impression that Texas was doing really well real estate wise and I had to inform her that we are doing well *compared to other markets*. She wants close to market, so I had to pass.

2. Financial Problems and Tenants That Are His Friends
[Source: Website]

A homeowner wants to sell a 3 bedroom, 1.5 bath, 1000-square-foot house in a so-so neighborhood.

Here are the numbers:

- Asking Price: $32,000
- Amount Owed: $20,000

- Repairs: Unknown (unconfirmed)
- After Repaired Value: $60,000
- Max Offer: $35,000 minus repairs

The seller is behind on payments on his own house, which is out of town, *and* his rental house in San Antonio. He has tenants in that are supposed to be gone by the end of the month. He is hesitant to send anyone in to see the house as the tenants were his friends and they were hoping to eventually buy the house (even though they've always been late with their rent. Go figure. Why is it not good to have your friends as tenants? Hmmm.)

He is two months behind on his payments and mentioned that he has contacted several people and will schedule with them to show it after the tenants are out. I'm not interested in this house but passed it on to someone I've informed of the situation. My investor should be able to work with the seller to contract this house before the tenants are out and avoid the competition that is likely to be waiting.

3. Nasty Divorce
[Source: Website]

This homeowner wants to sell a 3 bedroom, 2 bath, 1300-square-foot house is a good neighborhood.

Here are the numbers:

- Asking Price: $65,000
- Amount Owed: $45,000
- Repairs: Cosmetic (unconfirmed)
- After Repaired Value: $95,000
- Max Offer: $62,000 minus repairs

These sellers have recently gotten divorced and need to sell this house. They are also behind on payments. Sort of a perfect storm.

4. Bought Another House
[Source: Website]

This homeowner wants to sell a 3 bedroom, 2 bath, 1100-square-foot house is a decent neighborhood.

Here are the numbers:

- Asking Price: $55,000
- Amount Owed: $0
- Repairs: $10,000
- After Repaired Value: $90,000
- Max Offer: $48,500

The seller bought another house and is moving out of this one. They said it needs quite a bit of work, but were asking a reasonable price. I went to check it out.

The house was in decent shape and just needed bathroom updates, flooring, paint, new water heater, drywall repair, light fixtures and some other small things. I ended up offering $45,000 on the spot. The seller's ex-husband, who met me there, said that that would not work. They wanted to walk away with $55,000. I told him the most I could do would be $47,000. I need to stick to my figure because the days on market in this neighborhood are high and this house is a little smaller than most.

5. The Other Investor Was An @$$&%*#
[Source: Website]

The homeowner wants to sell a 4 bedroom, 2 bath, 1500-square-foot house is a decent neighborhood.

Here are the numbers:

- Asking Price: $80,000
- Amount Owed: $80,000
- Repairs: Quite a few (unconfirmed)

- After Repaired Value: $100,000
- Max Offer: $65,000 minus repairs

The seller recently got married and wants to sell this house fast to avoid the hassle of sitting on the market for months and having to do repairs. He had called another investor before me and he said the guy was extremely rude and really just an @ss. Competition is really not as bad as most of us believe it to be. After some research, I determined that I would not be able to buy the house because too much is owed. Next.

6. My Tires Have Been Kicked
[Source: Website]

The homeowner wants to sell a 4 bedroom, 2.5 bath, 3000-square-foot house is a good neighborhood.

Here are the numbers:

- Asking Price: $200,000
- Amount Owed: $145,000
- Repairs: Cosmetic (unconfirmed)
- After Repaired Value: $210,000
- Max Offer: $136,500

This seller wants to downsize and sell for nearly full market value. No thanks. There does not seem to be any motivation either and was just curious. That's understandable.

The seller called me back later when I was taking our twins to dance class. I had her on Bluetooth to my car and she was hard to understand, so I had to have her repeat herself. Basically, after our conversation, she got on Zillow and looked up her house value. She was shocked. Zillow showed $140k. She mentioned that a Realtor had just told her to list it for $230k only 30 days ago. She wanted to know what had happened to her neighborhood for the values to drop that dramatically in that short period of time.

Now, an unscrupulous investor would have taken this opportunity to really work a seller. Not cool. I informed her that Texas is a non-disclosure state, which means that sales of homes are not made public. Zillow can only guess at values based on loan amounts and whatever other random silliness they incorporate. I am really surprised that Zillow does not put huge disclaimers on their site for people accessing it from non-disclosure states.

She was relieved to hear about this. It felt good that she had called to ask me about this versus the Realtor she had talked to. Guess who built better rapport. Still no deal, but got a good story out of it. :)

--

Other leads this week (10 of them) weren't great. Mostly sellers owe too much for it to be worthwhile for me and a few others were too far out of town.

Active deals

Frustration House
We closed on the Frustration House yesterday. We met with our contractor there this morning and are awaiting his bid. This should be a quick rehab and we should be able to have it on the market within two weeks. You'll find updates in the coming weeks, but if you want to see how it turned out, flip to the Flipped Houses section.

Historic House
Finally, we bought and sold the Historic House. You can find the details of this house in the Flipped Houses section at the end of the book.

Next steps
- Have work started on the Frustration House.
- Push the Def Leppard House for sale.

Week 19

The Benefits of Flipping: Vacation

This week, I went to Oshkosh for Air Venture! This place is awesome. I have missed some leads this week due to wanting to completely relax and not be a slave to my phone. I bird-dogged most of the leads and next week we should see some more as I get into ones I missed, if they are still available.

Lead Analysis

Lead source	Number of leads
Yellow pages	2
Buying website	4
Probate	1
Total	**7**

1. Empty Nester, House Too Big
[Source: Yellow Pages]

The homeowner wants to sell a 3 bedroom, 2 bath, 1100-square-foot house in a decent neighborhood.

Here are the numbers:

- Asking Price: $60,000
- Amount Owed: $45,000
- Repairs: Cosmetic (unconfirmed)
- After Repaired Value: $75,000
- Max Offer: $48,000 minus repairs

The kids have moved out and the house is too big. I'm not sure how an 1100-square-foot house is too big, but oh well, maybe there is more to the story. They said it could use some painting. Since I'm not really interested in the area, I bird-dogged it.

2. Mother Passed, Inherited and Wants to Sell
[Source: Website]

This homeowner wants to sell a 3 bedroom, 1 bath, 800-square-foot house in a so-so neighborhood.

Here are the numbers:

- Asking Price: $50,000
- Amount Owed: $0
- Repairs: Cosmetic (unconfirmed)
- After Repaired Value: $70,000
- Max Offer: $45,000 minus repairs

The seller inherited the house when her mother passed last year. She was going to sell it then, but ended up with throat cancer. Now that she has recovered from treatment, she is ready to sell the house. There is a deal here, but I am not really interested in the house since I'm pretty busy. I know people interested in this area, so I bird-dogged it.

3. Want to Sell but Won't Give Address
[Source: Probate]

A homeowner I spoke to this week wants to sell a house but would not give me any information about it. How does this ever make sense to anybody? I guess there is a very real possibility that I may go over there and lift the house up and steal it... just hook some chains up to it and drag it down the street. Maybe bring a heavy-duty helicopter. Maybe some magical, vanishing pixie dust sprinkled here and there. Maybe I'll entice the house to follow me while I play my mythical unicorn flute... I have her number and will call again after a couple weeks. So ridiculous.

--

As you can see, I bird-dogged quite a few this week. The other 4 leads were just asking way too much and I didn't want to bother negotiating with the upcoming vacation.

Active deals

Hidden Iron House
We closed on the Hidden Iron House this week. You'll find a breakdown of the true numbers for the deal along with other details in the Flipped Houses section.

Def Leppard House
The Def Leppard House has been rehabbed, cleaned and staged, and is now on the market. We are currently negotiating an offer but are dealing with the 90 day FHA flip rule again. The buyer really wants to move in before the end of the summer, so we are checking to see if they would be okay with leasing the house for a month and then closing after the 90 days are up.

Frustration House
We have started the rehab on the Frustration House. The seller happened to be at the house the morning I met my contractor there. He continued to cement the name we came up with for the house by walking around following us while we were going over the scope of work. Every room we went into he would give his input on what he thought we should do. My contractor was getting confused as I was telling him what I wanted done and this guy was mentioning other contradictory things. He then went on to talk about how he should have waited to make the commitment to sell and how he knew we would make a fortune on the house. I'd heard enough of this and asked him if he had everything he was going to take from the house and opened the front door for him.

The next day, my contractor started work there. He called me in the morning and told me someone had gone in and removed the light bulbs out of the bathrooms and the red toilet seat. Strange. It must have been the seller.

Good old frustration house. It's not like we were going to keep the toilet seat anyway...it was red for heaven's sake!

My guy is doing the repairs for $5,500. I still need to have the carpet guy come in when this work is done and that should be about $2,000. My AC guy probably needs to replace the blower motor but he has not been there to verify yet. I'm sure there will be other miscellaneous items that pop up and I will let you know when they do. For a full description of the scope of work and the rehab numbers, check the Flipped Houses section.

Def Leppard House
We finally got approval from the HOA for our red door at the Def Leppard House. Great.

Next steps
- Check on Frustration House rehab.
- Enjoy the vacation!

Week 20

Flipping While on Vacation

My wife and I took the kids up to the greatest air show on earth in Oshkosh, Wisconsin. It was absolutely spectacular. You can probably guess who wanted to go there for vacation... We were hoping for a break from the south Texas heat, but it was hot up there as well.

We also went to Chicago and stayed downtown for three nights. My wife and I love Chicago. It was the first time for the kids to be there and they enjoyed it. We did the bus tour and a boat tour, Shedd Aquarium, Navy Pier, Sears Tower, and lots of walking. Due to wanting to not have many interruptions during our vacation, I missed a lot of calls. I tried to let as many people know as I could that I would call them when I got back. If they were in more of a hurry, I passed the lead on to an investor in San Antonio to look into. This week is short of at least 5-10 leads where people did not leave messages or call me back. This is exactly why it's so important to pick up the phone when someone calls you. You just never know if it's the one call you've been waiting for.

The time with my family uninterrupted was well worth it, though and I would handle things the same way next time. But when I am not on vacation, you better believe I am answering the phone whenever I have the chance.

We were in somewhat of a drought in Texas that season and we had some strict restrictions against watering lawns and other uses of water. The sprinkler system at one of the had been going off at a non-approved time, so we got a citation for it. We are closing on that house soon; hopefully, the grass doesn't die before then.

Lead Analysis

Lead source	Number of leads
Bandit signs	1
Buying website	11
Wholesale	1
Total	13

1. Divorced and Wife Abandoned the House
[Source: Website]

This homeowner wants to sell a 4 bedroom, 2 bath, 2100-square-foot house in a good neighborhood.

Here are the numbers:

- Asking Price: Make an offer
- Amount Owed: $100,000
- Repairs: Minor (unconfirmed)
- After Repaired Value: $130,000
- Max Offer: $85,000 minus repairs

The seller got divorced and his ex-wife was living in the house but has since abandoned it and now he needs to sell. The days on market in this neighborhood are high and too much is owed for me. This might work as a short sale or sub2 for someone.

2. Wholesale That I Looked at in 2007
[Source: Wholesale]

The homeowner wants to sell a 4 bedroom, 4 bath, 6666-square-foot house in a great neighborhood.

Here are the numbers:

- Asking Price: $380,000
- Amount Owed: Wholesale

- Repairs: Updated (unconfirmed)
- After Repaired Value: $500,000
- Max Offer: $325,000 minus repairs

A wholesaler called with this lead. It's a listed foreclosure that I had looked at back in 2007 when the owners still owned the house. This house is just plain *ugly*. The style is not appealing and the landscaping is nonexistent. It would take a lot of work to make this house sell for the ARV they are telling me ($700k+). The more realistic ARV is closer to $500k and I still think it would sit on the market a while. I think I had offered $300k back in '07 before the market decided to go south. If I was going to buy a house that cost that much, it would have to be a no-brainer. I'll have to pass.

3. Husband Transferring
[Source: Website]

This homeowner wants to sell a 3 bedroom, 2.5 bath, 2700-square-foot house in a good neighborhood.

Here are the numbers:

- Asking Price: $165,000
- Amount Owed: $0
- Repairs: Cosmetic (unconfirmed)
- After Repaired Value: $180,000
- Max Offer: $117,000 minus repairs

The husband is being transferred and they are checking to see what an investor would pay and then are going to consult with a Realtor. I didn't spend much time on this because I wasn't very confident in getting it. I made a ballpark offer of around $120,000 and let them know that I would need to verify what kinds of repairs would be needed. I'm not going to hold my breath.

--

Not much going on this week in terms of leads. The other 10 I got were asking way too much, owed too much, or were just too far outside my area.

Active deals

Frustration House
The rehab is progressing on the Frustration House. I initially did not include doing anything with the kitchen and bathroom floors. They were sheet vinyl and in good shape. After the house was finished, our Realtor mentioned how cheap the floors looked, so we are going to go ahead and put in ceramic tile in all wet areas.

Hidden Iron House
We've finally and officially closed on the Hidden Iron House. The final numbers and details can be found at the end of the book in the Flipped Houses section.

Next steps
- Order more bandit signs.
- Make follow-up calls.

Week 21

House Flipping Journey

This week took a little effort to get back into it after our vacation. I find myself slacking a little with the marketing and need to pick that back up. I should find a way to delegate it a little better.

I got a hold of about seven people in one day that I had talked to before. Nothing great, but you never know where these things will go. By keeping in touch with them, when they are finally ready to sell, they will think of me.

I also ordered 200 more bandit signs and I'll slowly put them out. An investor friend just told me he got fined for 11 signs ($150/each). I'm sure he can negotiate the fee, but I asked if they had warned him first and he said, "Not this time." So, be careful. People do get fined.

On a better note, my wonderful wife was at it again with another great article this week. A good team is vital to your success, so she's written about the people on our team who help with the business. You can read the bonus article online at http://www.flippingjunkie.com/2011/do-you-have-a-dream-house-flipping-team.

Lead Analysis

Lead source	Number of leads
Yellow pages	2
Buying website	5
Probate	3

Lead source	Number of leads
REO	1
Referral	1
Total	**12**

1. Inherited Needs Work
[Source: Probate]

This homeowner wants to sell a 2 bedroom, 2 bath, 1100-square-foot house in a so-so neighborhood.

Here are the numbers:

- Asking Price: Make an offer
- Amount Owed: Not much
- Repairs: Quite a bit (unconfirmed)
- After Repaired Value: $70,000
- Max Offer: $45,000 minus repairs

The seller inherited the house. She wouldn't tell me exactly how much was owed and seemed like she really wanted it to be sold easy, but did not want to do it easily. She wants to negotiate and play ball, but also be rid of the house quickly.

She wanted to know how much I would offer. I am not interested in a house in this area, so I just made a ballpark offer in the $30's to feel out whether she is motivated or not. She wasn't interested, but maybe she will be in a couple weeks.

2. Wants to Downsize
[Source: Yellow Pages]

The homeowner wants to sell a 4 bedroom, 2.5 bath, 3600-square-foot house in a great neighborhood.

Here are the numbers:

- Asking Price: $350,000
- Amount Owed: $0
- Repairs: Foundation and roof leak (unconfirmed)
- After Repaired Value: $400,000
- Max Offer: $260,000 minus repairs

The seller wants to downsize so he can travel and enjoy his retirement. This house is right down the street from another one we are currently working on. He did not seem at all motivated, but the more I talked to him the more I felt that maybe he was. He had mentioned selling his last house through a Realtor and was not happy that he ended up with just a little more than the "we buy ugly houses" people offered. Of course, he had to wait months and deal with all of the hassles of selling the conventional way, which is why he wasn't very happy.

He just wanted a ballpark to begin with, so I gave him one in the under-$250k range, depending upon the repairs of course. He said he would think about it and I will be following up.

3. Taking Care of Elderly Mom
[Source: Website]

The homeowner wants to sell a 4 bedroom, 2 bath, 1500-square-foot house in a decent neighborhood.

Here are the numbers:

- Asking Price: $70,000
- Amount Owed: $68,000
- Repairs: Cosmetic+ (unconfirmed)
- After Repaired Value: $110,000
- Max Offer: $71,500 minus repairs

The seller is taking care of his elderly mother and doesn't need this house. He just wants to get out from underneath it. My maximum offer would be just around what he owes, so when I went to the house and saw that there was about $10-12k in repairs needed, it became a no-go for me. I passed the lead on to another investor.

In the end, the investor lost out on the deal because he wasn't able to visit the house the same day I told him about it. You've got to be fast; you can't steal in slow motion.

4. Inherited and Need to Sell
[Source: Yellow Pages]

This homeowner wants to sell a 3 bedroom, 2 bath, 1100-square-foot house in a decent neighborhood.

Here are the numbers:

- Asking Price: $80,000
- Amount Owed: $0
- Repairs: $10,000
- After Repaired Value: $90,000
- Max Offer: $48,000 ($58,000 - $10,000)

This seller inherited the house. There are several heirs and one is living in the house. Before we talked much, I made sure that all were on board with selling it. I don't know how many times I've had people negotiate with me and get down to getting the deal done only to find out one of them didn't want to sell at all.

She said all were interested in selling, so I have analyzed the deal. I will need to get this one quite a bit below their asking price. I offered $43k and they said they were going to talk it over with the other people involved.

5. Parents Moving in With Them
[Source: Website]

The homeowner wants to sell a 5 bedroom, 3 bath, 2600-square-foot house in a good neighborhood.

134

Here are the numbers:

- Asking Price: Make an offer
- Amount Owed: $0
- Repairs: $43,000
- After Repaired Value: $135,000 (maybe $140k)
- Max Offer: $45,000 ($88,000 - $43,000)

The parents are moving out of this house and in with the caller. The house needs everything, according to the seller. This was a real hoarder house with stuff stacked everywhere. The best part was a sign on one of the bedroom doors that stated not to open it because there was a raccoon in the room. I asked the guy showing me if there really was a raccoon trapped in there at one time. He said, "Yes. It fell out of the ceiling over here in the living room and ran upstairs into that room." He then pointed at a hole in the ceiling.

The plan was for them to have three investors look at the house and make offers. This happens a lot and I don't like it because then everyone is playing the game of trying to find out what the other investors offered. I mentioned this problem to him so he could feel that we were on the same team. He then said that everyone just needed to give their highest and best and that there would be no second offers. This is why I offered my maximum.

When you know there will be other investors making offers, it can be tempting to wait until all of them have made offers and get the deal by offering just a little more. Don't do this. Sometimes the seller will see this as being sneaky. A lot of the time, they will not wait for all offers and will accept one on the spot. Make your offer and just work hard at building good rapport. That is most important.

--

In addition to these leads, I got another 7, most of which just didn't have the numbers to make them worthwhile for me.

Active deals

Frustration House

The Frustration House is nearing completion. We have the tile going in right now. Once that is done, the carpet guy will go in with new carpet. Then all we have to do is have it cleaned and staged.

The yard at that house looks pretty rough. The previous owner had dogs that tore it up and it is now mostly dirt. This severe drought we are having down here doesn't help. There is no way I am going have sod put down as it would never make it. We have watering restrictions and I don't feel like going over there every day or paying someone to do it. We will offer a credit for the new buyer to do as they wish.

Next steps

- Wrap up Frustration House rehabs.
- Get back in gear with mailings.
- Prepare another probate mailing.

Week 22

Finding Investments Properties from the Air

I went flying on Monday afternoon and spotted a lot of smoke close by. We flew over to see what it was (staying clear of the smoke mind you) and saw a house completely engulfed in flames and there were no firemen on site. It must have started very recently. It did not take but 30 minutes for it to completely burn to the ground.

We also had some strange goings on this week with regards to one of the houses we already had before this book. We've had it under contract to close for a month and everything was progressing smoothly. Then, after the inspection, we sent contractors to the house to repair items uncovered in the buyer's inspection report. Nothing major.

All of the repairs were done immediately and we quickly informed the buyer's agent of that fact. The closing was scheduled for Tuesday. On Monday evening, the buyers had a walkthrough and re-inspection of the items we repaired. It appears the electrician and roofer did not complete everything. Fine. Not a big deal — so we thought. We were waiting for a list from this agent and they decided not to give it to us until about an hour before the scheduled closing time. We had been begging for it all day so we could take care of the items right away.

It appeared we would be signing an extension and closing later this week, but that evening, we got a call from our agent informing us that the buyer is considering backing out and might even sue because we did not have the repairs done. What!?

I debated even adding this but it really makes my blood boil. That night, we got a termination of contract and release of earnest money document emailed to us alluding to the fact that we really should sign "or else." Ridiculous. If they wanted out of the contract, there are better ways to do it. So, this could end up being quite the fiasco. At this point, it is all a matter of principle and I don't personally like people who try to push us around. We will not let them.

In other news, one of my buyers is looking for a lot of properties in a certain area that I don't really market in anymore. I decided to get another list of absentee owners to mail postcards to. I ended up with a list of about 990 addresses. Combining those with the driving for dollars lists that I already had due for another mailing, it ended up being 1123 postcards.

I use click2mail.com to print and mail the cards. I went with the 5x8, black ink on yellow cardstock. The total ended up being $709 for printing and mailing first class.

With all of this going on, I am already falling behind on my mailings and need to get them off my plate, so I'm working on delegating them better. I'm now using an electronic signature on my mailings and I've put together a list of instructions for the sequence of letters and postcards and how often they get mailed. We are going to buy the person doing the work a laser printer so that she can print everything and mail them out herself.

One of the more important aspects of real estate investing is getting funding. I do this, most of the time, through private lenders. I've put together The Ultimate Guide to Finding and Approaching Private Lenders (which you can access at http://flippingjunkie.com/how-to-find-and-approach-private-lenders-the-ultimate-guide/) to help you with your house flipping journey.

As you can tell, this has been a busy week for me. I'm glad to have gotten my act back together with regards to the marketing and leads should be picking up in the coming weeks.

Lead Analysis

Lead source	Number of leads
Yellow pages	1
Buying website	7
Wholesale	1
Absentee owners	1
Total	**10**

1. Tenant Not Paying Rent [Front Yard Stink House]
[Source: Absentee Owner Postcards]

The homeowner wants to sell a 3 bedroom, 2 bath, 1000-square-foot house in a decent neighborhood.

Here are the numbers:

- Asking Price: Make an offer
- Amount Owed: $0
- Repairs: House in poor condition (unconfirmed)
- After Repaired Value: $65,000
- Max Offer: $40,000 minus repairs

The landlord called from a postcard I sent them months ago. They have a tenant they've evicted and would like to see what they could get for the house. They mentioned that it was in very bad shape. The sellers are in their 70's and don't want to deal with the hassles anymore. I am going to keep in touch with them and visit the house as soon as the tenant has vacated. This did end up becoming a deal, which you can follow along over the coming weeks. Details can be found in the Flipped Houses section as well. This one is the Front Yard Stink House.

2. Might Be Accepting Job Out of State
[Source: Website]

The homeowner wants to sell a 3 bedroom, 2 bath, 1600-square-foot house in a good neighborhood.

Here are the numbers:

- Asking Price: $159,000
- Amount Owed: $159,000
- Repairs: Nothing (unconfirmed)
- After Repaired Value: $155,000
- Max Offer: $100,000 minus repairs

This owner wants to find out how much she can get for the house. She just bought it two years ago and now is going to have trouble competing with the new houses in the neighborhood. The builders are offering great incentives to move houses and it is hard to compete with them. This is the reason for my lower ARV. Next.

3. Wholesaling House
[Source: Wholesaler]

This homeowner wants to sell a 3 bedroom, 2 bath, 1000-square-foot house in a decent neighborhood.

Here are the numbers:

- Asking Price: $52,000
- Amount Owed: Unknown
- Repairs: $20,000 (unconfirmed)
- After Repaired Value: $70,000
- Max Offer: $45,000 minus repairs

Look at those numbers. Do they make sense to anybody? I included the details on this one to show some of the bad leads I've been getting. The ARV that was given to me was $99k! No way. This is exactly why you cannot trust what anyone tells you a property is worth. You have to see the comparables yourself and make your own decision.

4. Residential Lot
[Source: Yellow Pages]

This homeowner wants to sell a vacant residential lot in a so-so neighborhood.

Here are the numbers:

- Asking Price: $7,000
- Amount Owed: $2,800
- Repairs: Nothing as this is just a vacant lot
- After Repaired Value: $7,000
- Max Offer: What is owed

This owner cannot afford the lot as he is behind on property taxes and owes the city for them having to mow the lot every year. I would only want this lot if he sold it to me for what is owed on it. I would then try to owner finance it and receive most of what I pay for the down payment.

--

This week, I got an additional 6 leads that didn't get anywhere — either the numbers didn't work or the area wasn't great. I did manage to pass one on to another investor, though.

Active deals

Frustration House
The Frustration House is almost done. The tile is almost finished and the carpet will be following, hopefully quickly. Early next week, we should have it cleaned and staged. Then, the most important part: it will be listed for sale.

Next steps

- Have the Frustration House staged and put on the market.
- Get some rest.

Week 23

Two More Under Contract

The frustrating incident regarding the sale of one of our existing houses has continued and it looks like we are heading to mediation. I'm not letting it stress me out because I know we are in the right. That is all that matters.

"I don't always go into mediation, but when I do, I prefer to stay positive. Stay positive my friends."
— The Most Interesting
House Flipper in the World

This week, I had 50 bandit signs put out in some new areas. There are 150 more that will go out about every other week.

I have also written two different probate letters and our mailing person is working on printing and stuffing the letters in envelopes. I'm going to test both letters at about 75 addresses each to see which one pulls better.

I got tons of leads this week. The postcard mailing really started pulling and I think there will be more coming over the next week. Bandit signs helped pull in some new leads as well. It really is all about keeping your marketing going and working the leads. Deals will come.

Lead Analysis

Lead source	Number of leads
Bandit signs	5
Yellow pages	2

Lead source	Number of leads
Buying website	6
Drive for dollars	1
Wholesale	1
Absentee owners	10
Total	**25**

1. Daughter Going Through Divorce [Honk the Horn House]
[Source: Website]

This homeowner wants to sell a 4 bedroom, 2 bath, 1500-square-foot house in a good neighborhood.

Here are the numbers:

- Asking Price: $75,000 (says the least they'll take is $70k)
- Amount Owed: $65,000
- Repairs: $15,000
- After Repaired Value: $120,000
- Max Offer: $80,000 minus repairs

The seller's daughter had been living in the house but is now going through a divorce and the house is vacant. It needs repairs and they don't want to mess with it. Smart move.

I went and saw the house and it wasn't too bad. I had to offer what he owes on the house and he did not hesitate to take it. I really enjoy these opportunities when they are just so relieved that you are going to buy the house so they don't have to mess with it. There really was no negotiating. I could only offer what he owed and he was happy to be done with it.

We signed the contract right then and there on the trunk of my car. The reason I'm calling this one the Honk the Horn House is because the seller's grandson was at the house with him and he wanted to pretend to drive the car. While we were signing the contract, he was constantly honking the horn and it was really pretty funny.

144

This one is under contract and set to close within about 2 weeks. I'll continue to update you on the progress of this deal over the next few weeks. You can find final details in the Flipped Houses section as well.

2. Husband Passed and Have Two Houses
[Source: Bandit Signs]

The homeowner wants to sell a 4 bedroom, 2 bath, 1600-square-foot house in a so-so neighborhood.

Here are the numbers:

- Asking Price: $80,000
- Amount Owed: $0
- Repairs: Cosmetic (unconfirmed)
- After Repaired Value: $75,000
- Max Offer: $48,000 minus repairs

The seller's husband passed away last year and she has this house that has been sitting vacant. The problem with the area is that there are houses built in the 60's (as was this one) and there are ones that were built over the last 5 years. All of these houses are competing for buyers and the ones from the 60's are not selling well.

I decided to give her a ballpark offer in the 40's to see if she would be interested. I did this over the phone because of how much she was asking. This can save you some time, although you might miss a deal here and there because when you meet them and make an offer in person, they start dropping their price.

One of the nice things about postcards and bandit signs is you don't have to worry so much about competition, so you can take your time with the deal and follow up later.

3. Are You Kidding Me!
[Source: Absentee Owner Postcards]

The homeowner wants to sell a 2 bedroom, 1 bath, 900-square-foot house in a not-so-good neighborhood.

Here are the numbers:

- Asking Price: $50,000
- Amount Owed: $0
- Repairs: Cosmetic (unconfirmed)
- After Repaired Value: $50,000
- Max Offer: $25,000 minus repairs

This seller told me that he wouldn't take less than $50k, but I wanted to see how he felt about a ballpark figure in the 20's. Big mistake in this situation. He was not at all happy and started in on a short but sweet rant.

4. 10 Acres with Oil
[Source: Yellow Pages]

A seller wants to sell 10 acres of land with mineral rights and oil. I'm looking into this one as I've never really dealt with this before. She says that they had pumped oil there for years but shut it down when the family was getting into disputes. Not sure what to think about that. More on this one next week.

I will leave you with what I told my wife when I mentioned this deal. I told her that if we bought and there did turn out to be oil, I would buy an old tank of a white Cadillac convertible and drive it to the land anytime I went down there. Would have to get horns for the hood as well.

When I talked to my attorney's office about a couple things, I mentioned that I might become an oil man and they asked if I meant in the oil fields or down at the Jiffy Lube! If I do get that Caddy, I will have to put a big Jiffy Lube magnet on the side.

5. Relocating Does Not Want to Sell Through Realtor
[Source: Website]

This homeowner wants to sell a 3 bedroom, 2.5 bath, 1700-square-foot house in a good neighborhood.

Here are the numbers:

- Asking Price: $80,000
- Amount Owed: $0
- Repairs: Minor foundation (unconfirmed)
- After Repaired Value: $100,000
- Max Offer: $65,000 minus repairs

The owner wants to relocate and does not want to deal with hassles of selling his house the conventional way. (I don't blame him!) I went to see this house and make an offer.

He called me about 10 minutes before our scheduled meeting telling me that he had a change of heart. I told him I was almost there and might as well see it and make him an offer. The house was built on a steep hill and was shifting down the hill. Nothing some piers wouldn't fix. They were not in a hurry to sell and had decided to go ahead and have the work done themselves. I told them that I would be in the 50's and let them know that if they changed their minds, they could call me.

--

This week I actually had six (yes, 6!) different owners ask ridiculous prices for their houses. These deals just can't work on my end, so of course I had to pass. All that in addition to 14 other leads this week, four of which I managed to pass on to another investor.

DANNY JOHNSON

Active Deals

A Big Decision

If you do not know about the rules regarding selling your home and capital gains, you really should keep reading and do some thinking. The rule is that if you live in a house (as your primary residence) any 2 of the 5 years prior to the sale, the first $250k ($500k if married) in profits is free from capital gains tax.

Basically, you won't have to pay federal taxes on the profit made from the sale. If you use the property as something other than your primary residence for the other years of ownership, the percentage of exclusion might change. With this in mind, my wife and I made a big decision this week.

My wife was over at the Expensive House (details of this deal have been removed from the book for privacy reasons) doing the staging on Tuesday. When she came home that afternoon, she told me she had something to ask me. She went on to ask how I felt about considering a move to that house. Immediately, my gut was telling me it was a great idea. Then, my brain had to get overly active and start considering all the pros and cons.

We decided to go over to the house and talk about it. About 4 hours from the time she got home and asked me, we had decided to go ahead and do it. We are moving into the house and will be putting ours up for sale. Now, because of the rule I told you about a second ago, we will not have to pay capital gains on the profit from the sale of our current house because we have just now lived in it for over two years. Lucky timing. This will be our third time doing this over the last 8 or so years.

Frustration House

The rehab on the Frustration House is just finishing up. The tile turned out really nice and I am glad we spent the money to do it. More details of what we did and the final numbers can be found in the Flipped Houses section.

Next steps

- Put the Frustration House on the market.
- Mail more postcards.
- Have contractors do minor repairs to our house so we can list it.

Week 24

The Halloweenists

Last week, I put the oil property (#4) under contract. My brother-in-law and I had gone out to see the property and found an overgrown lot with trees and heavy, thick brush. I questioned how oil trucks would have gotten to the back of the property, where the oil well was supposed to be, as late as 1999. The brush was just too thick and the trees looked to be older than that.

I immediately called the seller and she informed me that the trucks would access the holding tank from a road that ran behind the back of the property. I wasn't sure if we'd be able to pinpoint where the back of the property would be, so we decided to try to walk from the front of the house. We made it a couple acres by following the game trails, but it was really slow going.

Side note: Before going, she told me to be careful because of the Javelinas (pronounced have-a-leen-ahs). I thought she had said halloweenists. What!? I was immediately thinking that there was some weird Satan-worshiping cult out there. After asking her to clarify, I understood what she was talking about.

It was tough getting back there so we used the GPS to figure out where the back of the property was. We went around to a road that ran behind the property and spotted a large tank and decided that it must be it. The tank had not been used in a long time. We jumped the gate and walked around the property looking for where the well would have been and for any markings on the tank to determine what it was so I could look up how much oil the well had been producing before it was closed.

We walked all over the back of the property and wondered why there were a lot of beer cans and a volleyball net hung between two trees out in the middle of nowhere. I called the seller and asked about a second tank we spotted and the pump jack that was still there. She paused for a minute and then said that they were a part of the property also. Weird. Why would she not have told me about that to begin with? I became even more suspicious.

At this point, we figured we had enough info and were headed home. I quickly pulled up the satellite image of the property on Google Maps to see where we had been walking only to see that *we were on someone else's property!*

The front part was correct, but when we went to the back section, it was not the same property. There was no road going behind. She must have been talking about the side road that required you to go through yet another person's property to get to the back.

At this point, I needed to get a hold of the survey to get this all straightened out. My wife and I met her at her office and looked it over. It showed nothing of a well anywhere! And then she said she had decided to all of a sudden "throw in" an adjacent 5 acres. Weird.

Then, she says she was going over the contract and wanted to make sure that the $30k she owed would *not* be taken out of the proceeds from the sale. Of course they were. I had clearly informed her of that several times. She told me that she needed to buy a new car and it would cost her a "cool forty." Who says that unless they were prepared to say it? Too funny.

I quickly nipped that in the bud and told her that I would not do it. She then suggested splitting the $30k. No. At that point, I could see that this was a dead deal and we were wasting our time. I told her we were done. Sadly, there won't be a large white Cadillac convertible in my near future.

On a better note, I got tons of leads again this week. I'm beginning to wonder if just mailing postcards is the way to go. The letters aren't pulling very well in comparison and they are cheap and easier to get mailed out.

I had 50 bandit signs put out last weekend and they certainly grabbed some attention — just from the wrong audience. Code compliance called me twice on Saturday. There were doubts about whether it really was someone who worked for the city, but my doubts went away after they gave me their office number. It seems unlikely that it was another investor just trying to minimize competition. I'm going to lay low for a little while as my friend also got three calls on the same day.

I wanted to bring something else to your attention. A lot of people assume that house flippers mostly buy from people facing foreclosure. After reading this book, it should be apparent that this is not the case at all. The reason I bring it up is because your marketing should be focused on who would need what you are offering. There are a lot of different reasons why people want to get rid of houses fast and this book shows you who they typically are. Focus on that and you should be well ahead of your competition.

Lead Analysis

Lead source	Number of leads
Bandit signs	4
Yellow pages	2
Buying website	9
Wholesale	1
Absentee owners	7
Probate	2
Total	**25**

1. Don't Want to Fix It Themselves
[Source: Website]

The homeowner wants to sell a 3 bedroom, 2.5 bath, 1400-square-foot house in a decent neighborhood.

Here are the numbers:

- Asking Price: $50,000
- Amount Owed: $16,000
- Repairs: $18,000

- After Repaired Value: $90,000
- Max Offer: $40,000 ($58,000 - $18,000)

This house needs repairs that the owners do not want to do themselves. They'd rather sell the house and be done with it. Their balance is low enough to where a deal is possible, so I went to see the house and make an offer.

The house looks good on the outside but bad on the inside. This thing is going every which way and needs to be leveled. Next door is a rental with a lot of trash in the yard. I ended up offering $38,000 because they said they have another investor coming by next week. Why would it take the other investor a week to see the house?

2. Out of State Heirs
[Source: Yellow Pages]

The homeowners want to sell a 3 bedroom, 2 bath, 1100-square-foot house in a so-so neighborhood.

Here are the numbers:

- Asking Price: Make an offer
- Amount Owed: $0
- Repairs: A lot (unconfirmed)
- After Repaired Value: $70,000
- Max Offer: $45,000 minus repairs

This is an inherited house with three heirs who all live out of state. There is someone living in the house who is related somehow. I was surprised when they told me they found me from the Yellow Pages. They had someone locally look in the book and call them with my number. You would think hopping on Google would be easier. This just goes to show you that people still use that big yellow book. She also mentioned me having to call long distance to them in another state. I haven't even heard that phrase used in years. We truly take our cell phones for granted.

I don't really like the area, though, so I bird-dogged it to another investor. Easy money.

3. Want Cash Offer Before Listing
[Source: Bandit Signs]

A homeowner wants to sell a 4 bedroom, 2.5 bath, 2200-square-foot garage in a good neighborhood.

Here are the numbers:

- Asking Price: Make an offer
- Amount Owed: $130,000
- Repairs: None (unconfirmed)
- After Repaired Value: $140,000
- Max Offer: $91,000 minus repairs

This seller has a Realtor going over to sign a listing agreement tomorrow. They wanted to see what we would offer. This is one of those cases where the seller is praying and hoping that I'll offer them some great price for their house. I'm sure they're thinking it is too good to be true, but let's cross our fingers. I quickly worked up a ballpark figure and informed them to go ahead with the listing because I can't touch it. Next.

4. Sad Situation
[Source: Probate]

The homeowner wants to sell a 4 bedroom, 2 bath, 1700-square-foot house in a good neighborhood.

Here are the numbers:

- Asking Price: Make an offer
- Amount Owed: $120,000
- Repairs: Cosmetic (unconfirmed)
- After Repaired Value: $135,000
- Max Offer: $88,000 minus repairs

This seller called while we were taking one of our daughters to dance class. I had the call on Bluetooth so that I could talk and drive (and everyone in the car could hear the conversation). She mentioned receiving a letter from me about buying any property an estate might need to sell. She quickly and angrily asked how I got her address and deceased husband's name. My hand went for the disconnect button and hovered there as I waited for the explosion of anger and cursing.

Thank God, it never came. It was really a sad situation and you could tell that she was trying to sell the house and deal with her loss and having a hard time. To me, these calls are harder to receive than the super angry ones.

Another investor had offered her in the 70's and she informed me of how much she owed. There is just nothing I could do in this situation. I'd love to help, but it just doesn't make financial sense. At least she has enough equity to sell it through a Realtor.

--

The other 21 leads from this week were a lot of tire kickers and a few who owed too much. I did, however, manage to bird-dog 10 properties this week.

Active deals

Frustration House
The Frustration House has been staged and cleaned.

Next steps

- Attempt to focus on business while having work done on our new house.

Week 25

Happy for Another Deal Under Contract

This week, the guy I had pulling probate leads for me called and said he would no longer be able to do so. Crud. This is not good. I guess I will have to look for someone else.

I was going to put out more bandits, but there has been too much anti-bandit sign activity lately. I'll have to lay low for another couple of weeks. Our relationship with the person that puts them out is also a little strained at the moment — don't ever, *ever* sell a house with owner financing to someone you know, even a contractor.

Despite the frustrations with probate and bandit signs, we still have quite a few leads coming in. I actually hesitated to send out more postcards this week so I could catch up a little and knew I would be spending time dealing with getting our next house ready for move-in.

Lead Analysis

Lead source	Number of leads
Bandit signs	1
Buying website	11
Wholesale	1
Absentee owners	5
Probate	1
Total	**19**

1. Estate Sale [Audi House]
[Source: Website]

An estate wants to sell a 4 bedroom, 2.5 bath, 2200-square-foot house in a good neighborhood.

Here are the numbers:

- Asking Price: Make an offer
- Amount Owed: Nothing
- Repairs: $28,000 (foundation, drywall, cosmetic)
- After Repaired Value: $150,000
- Max Offer: $69,000 ($97,000 - $28,000)

This house was in a nice pocket of the neighborhood. It needs updating throughout and foundation work, but it would be a good buy. I offered $65k and the seller didn't seem shocked and said he would talk it over with the family. We continued to talk about some things and I was trying to treat the conversation as though we had already made an agreement.

Later in the week, we got a verbal acceptance on this one and it did end up being a deal. You can follow along with the Audi House in the coming weeks and find final deal information in the Flipped Houses section at the end of the book.

2. Very Tired Landlord Wholesaler
[Source: Wholesale]

A homeowner wants to sell a 2 bedroom, 1 bath, 800-square-foot house in a not-so-good neighborhood.

Here are the numbers:

- Asking Price: $40,000
- Amount Owed: $35,000
- Repairs: Everything
- After Repaired Value: $60,000
- Max Offer: $35,000 minus repairs

This is from a wholesaler I have known for a while. He has this rental and just wants to get rid of it. I've had and still have houses like this and know exactly how he feels. Unfortunately, he isn't able to sell it for what I would need to get it for.

When I went to see this one, the tenant was home drinking lots of beer before noon. Not sure he does much other than that based on the state of the house, even though he knew I was coming to see it. Of course, a lot of tenants will do things to keep landlords from selling because they don't want to be thrown out.

3. Father's House
[Source: Probate]

The homeowner wants to sell a 2 bedroom, 1 bath, 800-square-foot house in a decent neighborhood.

Here are the numbers:

- Asking Price: $55,000
- Amount Owed: $0
- Repairs: Cosmetic and bathroom repairs (unconfirmed)
- After Repaired Value: $50,000
- Max Offer: $25,000 minus repairs

This seller inherited his father's house and wants to sell because he doesn't want to be a landlord and could use the money to finish up the repairs on his own house. He is asking a high price, but I will have to tell him that I will need to buy below $30k and see where he is at.

Side note: It seems like the sincere letter is pulling better. I don't think there have even been any calls from the nonspecific letter.

--

This week, I got 16 other leads. I wasn't able to get in touch with some of them and others either owed too much or were in bad neighborhoods. I did manage to bird-dog a few, though.

Active deals

Honk Your Horn House
We were supposed to close on the Honk Your Horn House today but ran into a problem. It was a pretty big problem, actually. I had made my offer in an amount that should have allowed the seller to not have to come to the table with any money at the closing. Unfortunately, the amount of taxes owed was quite a bit higher than we had anticipated.

The title company has to withhold a certain amount for property taxes because the seller had a homestead exemption on it for the last five years and he was not living there, and this put us over by quite a bit.

I talked it over with the seller and was attempting to see if he would be able to come to the closing with the difference. He was getting anxious and told me he would call me back. When he did, it was not what I wanted to hear. The talk was now starting in the direction of him backing out, so we went back to negotiating.

This is how it went: Can you pay half? No. What are you going to do? Keep making payments on it. How much are your payments? $800. Ok, how about you pay $800 and I will pick up the rest? (Did I just say that? Darn it.) Actually, it was the only thing I could do to salvage the deal without having to pay the full amount. We should be alright still.

Front Yard Stink House
This one was from Week 22. The seller was having difficulty getting the tenant out of the house, but I was finally able to see it the other day. The place was trashed but very fixable. It smelled really, really bad, but I'm sure that was just the week-old food sitting out on the counter and the nasty water in the sink.

The tenant actually showed up at the house while we were there. He did not look either of us in the face and I can understand why. I stayed out front with the seller to keep him company while the tenant was getting some of his stuff. The seller asked when he would have all of his stuff out and the tenant mumbled something about five days.

I immediately thought they had been way too lenient with this guy. His stuff should have already been out on the curb at this point. I don't mean to sound harsh, but this guy has been taking advantage of the seller for who knows how long. He's trashed the house and was being somewhat disrespectful.

I worked up the numbers while sitting in my car in front of the house and then called after running a couple more errands. I offered $20k and she quickly told me that her husband would never go for anything that low. She then asked if there was room for negotiating and I told her that the offer was so low that I didn't build any room in for negotiating (which was actually the case).

They called me back that same evening and told me that if they netted $20k they would be willing accept the offer.

The next morning, I got busy with a bunch of little things and was just about to call them when they called me. They wanted to get this thing over with and told me they were willing to net $19,000. Sure, I was willing to do that.

This one should close within a couple of weeks. I'm debating on whether to try and wholesale this house or fix it up and sell it with owner financing.

Next steps

- Close on the Honk Your Horn House.
- Send out some more postcards.
- Attempt to focus on business while having work done on the new house.

Week 26

Two More Deals Signed Up

Finding a good contractor can be very, very frustrating and very, very time-consuming. Once you find a good one though, your life can become a lot easier. Be sure to invest the time up front. I use the term invest because you really are trying to spend time now so that less of your time is consumed and wasted in the future.

We have been having some issues with our current contractor who we've been using for at least 3 or 4 years now. It's been nice being able to call him to send him to do quick jobs on houses and get the bill later because I know he will not submit ridiculous bills. We've gotten into a rhythm with the rehabs as he knows that I will not accept high bids and we don't waste each other's time. The issue we're having now relates to workmanship — too many small things have been popping up that were done out of pure laziness and I wonder if some mistakes were made on purpose.

I really should have spent the time months ago looking for a new contractor, but I know how hard it can be to find a good one and I have been taking the easy way out and avoiding it. It's now come to the point where I need to go ahead and invest the time in finding someone new.

All week, I've been making calls to other investors and talking to several contractors. The ones I felt best about met me at the Honk Your Horn House yesterday to talk and go over the scope of work. While going through this I thought it would be helpful to provide an article about the process. You can read the bonus article online at http://flippingjunkie.com/how-to-find-and-interview-contractors-for-your-rehabs/.

Apart from that, we got all the old tile out (almost 10,000 pounds worth!) of our house. We also had the master bath plumbing and electrical rough-ins done, and sheetrock hung. The fireplace and master bath will be tiled soon as well.

In terms of marketing, I mailed another 480 5x7 postcards out to absentee owners using click2mail.com and posted an ad on Craigslist. I have not done this in a really long time and figured it wouldn't hurt to try it again as it only takes a couple of minutes. I've already gotten a call from it this week, so I'll have to try to keep posting ads.

Mondays are usually my most hectic day. I think a lot of people look for investors to call about selling their house on the weekend, but wait to call until Monday. I got 13 or more leads this week *just on Monday*! My head was spinning by the end of the day. Things are really rolling now and we are going to get pretty busy, especially with the upcoming move.

Lead Analysis

Lead source	Number of leads
Yellow pages	5
Buying website	12
Wholesale	1
Probate	1
Craigslist	1
Total	**20**

1. Aunt Passed Away [Perp House]
[Source: Website]

The homeowner wants to sell a 3 bedroom, 1 bath, 1100-square-foot house in a so-so neighborhood.

Here are the numbers:

- Asking Price: Make an offer
- Amount Owed: Nothing

- Repairs: $8,000
- After Repaired Value: $60,000
- Max Offer: $35,000 minus repairs

The seller inherited this house from her aunt who recently passed away. The house is a newer one in an older neighborhood and would make a good rental or owner-financed house. My ARV was for retail sale and that would take a while with the high days on market in the area. If I sold it with owner financing, I could sell for much more. The house didn't need much beyond some leveling, so I offered $30,000. They did not like that offer, but this one ended up becoming a deal. More details to follow.

2. Moved to Different School District
[Source: Website]

This homeowner wants to sell a 4 bedroom, 2 bath, 1900-square-foot house in a good neighborhood.

Here are the numbers:

- Asking Price: $190,000
- Amount Owed: $150,000
- Repairs: Flooring and cosmetic (unconfirmed)
- After Repaired Value: $215,000
- Max Offer: $140,000 minus repairs

The seller moved to another area to change school districts. The school district the house is in isn't bad, so I guess it was for other reasons. Just a little too much is owed on this one and the seller is asking too much for me to be interested.

I told him I would be below what he owes but know another investor who would probably get somewhere just above what is owed, but he was firm on his asking price. This is when I asked him again what the lowest is that he'd be willing to accept. He mentioned $180k and I don't know anyone that could make it work for that much.

3. Helping Sister Sell Her House
[Source: Website]

A homeowner wants to sell a 3 bedroom, 2 bath, 1300-square-foot house in a decent neighborhood.

Here are the numbers:

- Asking Price: $80,000
- Amount Owed: $0
- Repairs: Cosmetic (unconfirmed)
- After Repaired Value: $80,000
- Max Offer: $50,000 minus repairs

The seller's sister called to see if I would make an offer on the house. They were asking for full market value and did not seem to need to sell right away, so I made a ballpark offer around the MAO and said it just depends on the repairs. This way, if the seller is negotiable enough to sell around where I would need to be, I will go and see it and try to work a deal.

This sort of situation may not have motivated sellers right away, but they may eventually become motivated enough. That is exactly what the motivated seller lead manager is for (available at flippilot.com).

4. Seller Wants to Downsize
[Source: Website]

This homeowner wants to sell a 3 bedroom, 2.5 bath, 2800-square-foot house in a good neighborhood.

Here are the numbers:

- Asking Price: $115,000
- Amount Owed: $56,000
- Repairs: Nothing (unconfirmed)
- After Repaired Value: $135,000
- Max Offer: $88,000 minus repairs

166

This seller just wants to downsize. She had the house listed for about 3 months at a super high price and then dropped it dramatically down to $145k for a couple weeks before canceling the listing. She said she'd only had two showings and no offers. Just with that, you can figure that the ARV is going to be at or below the $145k. After looking at comparable sales, I feel $135k is much more likely. Of the ones that sold, days on market were pretty high.

With the dramatic price decrease and now asking $115k, she must have some motivation.

5. Beat Cancer but Cannot Find a Job
[Source: Yellow Pages]

The homeowner wants to sell a 3 bedroom, 2 bath, 1700-square-foot house in a decent neighborhood.

Here are the numbers:

- Asking Price: $105,000
- Amount Owed: $98,000
- Repairs: Cosmetic (unconfirmed)
- After Repaired Value: $109,000
- Max Offer: $70,000 minus repairs

This seller was diagnosed with cancer a few years ago, but he was recently told that there were no more signs of it. I was glad to hear that. The problem is that he cannot find a job, even an entry-level one. This is making it so he can't afford his house any longer.

This is truly a situation where I wish I could just pay his house off and help him out, but I can't. I bring this up because you will face a lot of situations like this when flipping houses and you will be mighty tempted to help, especially when the numbers are closer to what your maximum offer is. There will be times where you will be $10k or $5k or even $3k off and you will be very, very tempted to fudge the numbers a little to make it work. Please avoid it. You will be glad you did. Do not make other peoples' problems your problem — this is especially true with contractors.

It may sound harsh, but it is a rule that I firmly believe will keep you out of a lot of trouble.

--

The other 15 leads from this week just didn't have the numbers I'd need to buy — either asking too much or owing too much. Some of the ones in bad neighborhoods I was able to bird-dog, though.

Active deals

Honk Your Horn House

We finally closed on the house this week. Our contractor has started work for $11,000. We will still need to pay my carpet guy separately, though. Details of our progress will follow and final numbers can be found in the Flipped Houses section.

Audi House

I got this one from last week (#1) under contract. The seller inherited the house and lives in Austin. He knew the house needed quite a bit of work and did not want to mess with it. They quickly accepted my offer and I met with him to sign it up on Monday morning. I think we talked more about cars than we did about the house.

This one should be a great flip. I'm tempted to wholesale it, as it does require quite a bit of rehab, so I'll follow up with you on how it goes in the coming weeks. Final numbers and deal details can be found in Flipped Houses near the end of the book.

Perp House

This second deal is one I analyzed earlier this week (#1). It will be a wholesale because my wife does not like the area. We had one for sale there a couple of years ago and it turned into a nightmare property. It took about a year to sell, got vandalized, and had an incident with kids breaking in and sleeping there.

In that case, my wife and our make-ready crew were meeting there to clean it as it had been on the market for a while. My wife went in and a teenager was inside the house. She asked him what he was doing there and he paused and then mentioned that he was interested in the house and was looking at it. He then mentioned that he was going to leave and, being as tough as she is, she told him that he was not going to and that she was going to call the police.

The perp was not going to stick around for that, so he decided to run out the front door. The problem was that my wife was standing between him and the door and she was holding our new-born baby in her car seat. He actually shoved her aside and took off running down the street.

One of the cleaners, even being over 50 (I know that's not old, but the kid was in his teens!), took off after him. My wife said it was actually sort of comical as the kid had saggy drawers and they kept falling down and he was struggling to keep them on. This allowed the cleaner giving chase to keep up with him a little, even as he was having to pause for breath. The kid made it through a drainage ditch that ran between two houses and outside the neighborhood to some neighboring apartments.

Here is the craziest part: the cleaner did not see where the kid had gone but assumed he must have run into the apartment upstairs where a bunch of crazy looking teenagers were hanging outside. He immediately went up and just entered the apartment. He found the kid and dragged him out. Awesome.

The police quickly arrived and took the kid into custody. My wife was really shaken up by the incident and I was extremely pissed. The police took it very seriously because they considered it assault of a child because my wife was holding our baby. Lesson learned: be careful going into vacant houses, even ones you own.

Anyway, that is why we are not going to buy the house with any intention of selling on a new loan. I will do my best to make a good profit by wholesaling it. If by chance I do not get a decent offer, I will sell the house with owner financing.

Front Yard Stink House
If you recall, this house had a terrible smell inside as the tenant had food and garbage everywhere. Well, this week we made a fresh new discovery.

I took my wife over to see the house yesterday and she was standing about 15 feet away in the middle of the front yard while I went in to make sure nobody was in the house. Even from that far away, she could smell it.

After clearing the house, I signaled for her to come inside and she refused. The smell was just too much! It's from the stuff in the sink. I should probably have someone do something about that before we close. Good stuff.

Next steps

- Close on the Front Yard Stink House.
- Send out some more postcards.
- Get the new house closer to move in.

Week 27

Contractor Quest

The journey continues in my attempt to find another good contractor. I had met several last week and one contractor stood out and seemed like he would be a good fit.

His estimate came in a couple grand high, but he accepted my counter bid for the Honk Your Horn House and we agreed to meet at a restaurant to go over my contract and get the paperwork so that he could get started the next day.

This is where my patience was tried. It seems like I have less and less patience these days. First, he was about 30 minutes late. I accepted this because I called him with little notice as to when I could be there, so not really a big deal. He was off in his estimate of when he could be there though. Splitting hairs?

He sat down and started to read my contract and the scope of work, which was not drawn up when we went over the job. I was very patient with him while he was going over the contract because I wanted to make sure he read the whole thing and that we were clear on everything that it states.

The key points of the contract being:

- He will be an independent contractor, not an employee.
- He agrees to do all work described in the scope of work in a professional manner and use the materials specified in the materials specification.
- The cost of the job, including materials.

- That they are expected to keep a clean job site.
- That I have to approve all work to my standards.
- All change orders will be in writing with accepted time estimates and cost estimates before any additional work is performed.
- I have every right to cancel the job if I am not satisfied at any point.
- A penalty is given if the work is not done by the deadline (with consideration given to weather and other delays).
- He warrants the work performed for at least a year.

He started to hesitate as he read my materials specification. Specifically, the cost of the bathroom vanities. The vanities cost $199 each at Home Depot. He informed me that I told him they would cost $59 each when going over the work at the house, which is a perfect example of why you should have your scope of work ready *before* you meet contractors — shame on me.

At this point, he started crunching numbers while hiding them with his folder. Very sneaky. Not sure what kind of math equations he was trying to solve as it took him nearly 20 minutes to crunch whatever numbers he was crunching. After I'd had enough of this secret number crunching, I informed him that I was busy and that he needed to pick up the pace a little. I had figured he was starting to become concerned about how much I was going to control the job and was thinking it through while writing numbers in his binder. Maybe he was just trying to figure out the pay for his guys based on the work and time, although this is something he should have done before agreeing to my price over the phone and possibly why he was throwing out wild numbers for the materials.

By now we had been sitting there for about an hour. He then mentioned that he understands I have things to do and that he would look over everything at home and call me to schedule meeting at the job to get started the next day. I told him that if I did not hear from him that night, I would assume he did not want the job. He assured me that he wanted the job and that he just needed to go over the contract again. I never heard from him.

I didn't wait long and called more contractors to meet with. This is an ongoing process that I wish was easier. But again, spend the time up front to find the right person so that you don't have a lot of problems during the project and end up having to fire someone.

At our house, the tiling is nearly completed and looks awesome! The wood floors will then go down, the vanities and bath fixtures will be installed, shower glass will be ordered and we will be set to move in. I do still have to call the home alarm company, the cable and Internet provider, family to help move, get boxes...oh man, what have we gotten ourselves into again?

Leads were steady throughout the week this week. I've slowed down a little on the marketing because I need to get existing rehabs underway and then get the new house ready and coordinate that move in. Lots of work ahead of us for the next couple of weeks.

Lead Analysis

Lead source	Number of leads
Bandit signs	1
Buying website	11
Wholesale	1
Probate	1
Craigslist	1
Referrals	1
Total	**16**

1. Wholesale Priced Too High

[Source: Wholesaler]

A wholesaler wants to assign a contract for a 3 bedroom, 2 bath, 1500-square-foot house in a decent neighborhood.

Here are the numbers:

- Asking Price: $67,000
- Amount Owed: $64,000 (under contract for)

- Repairs: $12,000 (based on pictures)
- After Repaired Value: $95,000
- Max Offer: $50,000 ($62,000 - $12,000)

This one is a wholesaler. The problem with this is that the comparable sales that have sold recently were all rehabbed very nicely with more than what we typically do for this price range house. I had to adjust either the ARV or the repair costs to make it accurate. I adjusted the repair cost to reflect the higher cost in doing more to the house and the numbers just don't work no matter how you slice it.

2. Divorced and Moving
[Source: Website]

The homeowner wants to sell a 3 bedroom, 2 bath, 1600-square-foot house in a decent neighborhood.

Here are the numbers:

- Asking Price: $95,000
- Amount Owed: $53,000
- Repairs: Cosmetic (unconfirmed)
- After Repaired Value: $90,000
- Max Offer: $59,000 minus repairs

This is a divorce situation and the seller just wants to get away from the house and all of the memories. This one was through my website and the seller only provided an email address as contact information, so I emailed them. When the seller responded, I gave a ballpark they were apparently offended by and demanded to know why I would need to buy it so low. They were politely informed that I cannot pay full market value and so on and so forth. I also felt it prudent to inform them that tone is always hard to convey by email and that I was not trying to be rude. It would have helped had they given a phone number so I could call them. No go.

3. Don't Want Hassle of Selling Through Realtor
[Source: Website]

A homeowner wants to sell a 3 bedroom, 2.5 bath, 1700-square-foot house in a good neighborhood.

Here are the numbers:

- Asking Price: $115,000
- Amount Owed: $102,000
- Repairs: $4,000 (carpet, exterior trim, tile)
- After Repaired Value: $140,000
- Max Offer: $87,000 ($91,000 - $4,000)

This one was a tricky one. The seller called me while I was headed out this morning to take care of business at several houses. He mentioned that another well-known investor in town had made an offer a couple of weeks ago and he had accepted it. The problem was that the investor was out of town at the time, so he had to wait until he got back to get the contract signed.

The seller then started making plans as if the house was already sold. He put an offer in on another house and had mentally made the leap and separated himself from his house. It was sold. He had already moved on. Then his world was shattered when the investor came back from out of town and informed him that he was unable to buy the house at this point.

The seller was clearly motivated to be done with the house when he called me. I guess he was having trouble accepting that his house was not, in fact, sold and still very much his problem. I was able to squeeze in a showing of the house between my appointments and saw the house. It did not need very much at all.

As I was looking at the numbers, I kept wondering why the other investor had backed out and started doubting my quick analysis of the comparables. I called an investor friend and asked him to run comparable sales for me and give me his opinion. He figured that $150k-$160k was safe.

175

Even with these numbers, the deal would have been tighter than I'd like, but I figured I could find someone to want it at just above what he owed. My gut kept telling me to recheck the comparable sales more closely though, as the other investor had backed out without reason.

When I got home, I checked again and realized this was a case where a thorough review of the comparable sales was necessary. The houses in the neighborhood were very similar but there was a bigger than normal difference between prices for single story and two-story houses. The singles were selling for about $100/sf and the two-story houses were selling for about $80/sf. That's a big difference!

He wants it paid off and would not consider sub2. I'll have to pass on this one.

--

I got 13 other leads this week. Most wouldn't work because of the numbers, but I did manage to pass a few on to other investors.

Active deals

Front Yard Stink House
Finally closed the Front Yard Stink House. I'll continue including updates on the rehab and resale of this one in the coming weeks. Final deal details will be in the Flipped Houses section.

Next steps
- Get estimates for work at the Front Yard Stink House.
- Send out some more postcards.

Week 28

Old Lead Under Contract

The journey continues in my attempt to find another good contractor for the rehabs on the houses we are flipping. I had another contractor I was willing to work with and we agreed on a price. He was happy to be getting the work. After telling him that we would have to meet first thing in the morning on Monday, he just acknowledged but then continued talking. Do not cut them off when they start rambling. Just be quiet and listen. He started mentioning some things that concerned me. Mainly, that he had just finished a big job for a church and he was waiting for payment and therefore could not buy any materials and needed money up front.

This could be a valid problem, but I believe it is probably a normal situation for contractors that have been out of work for a little while. They are behind on their bills., which is understandable and I can't fault them for that. The problem is when they receive some money for materials up front and it either goes to finish a job they haven't finished yet or to pay their bills. They begin with you upside down and it is never pleasant. I'm not saying this is always the case, but I'd err on the side of caution.

I was still going to meet with him and go over the contract. The draw schedule was set up so that there was less chance of becoming upside down on the job. The payments would be smaller and based on work already done.

My schedule was busy and I had to get up early to be able to meet with him. He wasn't there on time and then called ten minutes late to tell me that his alarm did not go off. Already with the excuses and we had not even started. This was a deal killer for me. It's too soon to have issues and it is usually a sign of how things will always be with him.

So, now I am back to square one. Not a big deal. I feel relieved that I avoided a dud.

At home, we have boxes everywhere and still a ton of stuff to box up. I was just thinking how funny it is that we pay big money for houses and then do our best to get boxes for free. Just can't see paying money for new boxes. We hit the jackpot yesterday by chance.

Lead Analysis

Lead source	Number of leads
Bandit signs	2
Yellow pages	2
Buying website	8
Absentee owners	1
Total	**13**

1. Moving to Take Care of Mother
[Source: Yellow Pages]

A homeowner wants to sell a 3 bedroom, 1.5 bath, 1100-square-foot house in a so-so neighborhood.

Here are the numbers:

- Asking Price: $35,000
- Amount Owed: $23,000
- Repairs: $15,000
- After Repaired Value: $70,000
- Max Offer: $30,000 ($45,000-$15,000)

The seller is moving in with his mom to take care of her. He mentioned that the house was already being made ready for sale, but they hadn't finished. He made it sound like it was nice and just needed minor touch ups.

I went out to see it and was surprised by the stink. I'm sorry, but the house really reeked of dog. There were giant rat holes chewed through the walls. Everything needed to be redone. I think the only things that looked fine were the roof and water heater.

He was not interested in my offer of $25,000. I really did not want to go above that. The room was there for another investor, so I bird-dogged it to see if he could make it work.

2. Has Other Houses and Cannot Afford
[Source: Yellow Pages]

The homeowner wants to sell a 3 bedroom, 3 bath, 2200-square-foot house in a not-so-good neighborhood.

Here are the numbers:

- Asking Price: $135,000
- Amount Owed: $87,000
- Repairs: Cosmetic (unconfirmed)
- After Repaired Value: $85,000
- Max Offer: $55,000 minus repairs

This seller cannot afford all of his houses and wants to get rid of this two-story one because they are having trouble going up and down the stairs. The house is in a rough area and he has an over-inflated idea of its value. No deal here or with any of his other houses. Next.

3. Willing to Come to the Table with Money
[Source: Website]

This homeowner wants to sell a 3 bedroom, 2 bath, 1000-square-foot house in a bad neighborhood.

Here are the numbers:

- Asking Price: $20,000
- Amount Owed: $24,000

179

- Repairs: A lot (unconfirmed)
- After Repaired Value: $35,000
- Max Offer: $10,000 minus repairs

The area this house is in is very bad. You can tell just by the fact that she immediately mentioned being willing to come to the table with $4k+ to help sell the house (because she owes $24k). I don't want it and sent it out to several investors and nobody wants to touch it. This is the type of property you need to buy in the low teens.

--

The other 10 leads this week were a mixture of tire kickers, people who owed too much and bad neighborhoods. I bird-dogged a few, but they were just not for me.

Active deals

Flatulent House
This week, I got a call from a guy that has a house he's been trying to sell for a while. I had actually looked at it several months ago and made an offer. He just recently decided to list it with a Realtor and has only received one showing. He is moving out of the country and just wants to have it gone.

He called to tell me that he was willing to take my offer, if it still stood. I could not remember the house, even after looking at the pictures I had taken, so I went back to see it and decided that it was still a deal. The comparable sales had to be checked again because it had been so long and a lot can change quickly in this market.

The seller wanted to have it close within 3 days and we didn't sign the contract until almost 5 that afternoon. I had to scramble. As soon as I left his house, I was making calls to get everything lined up. So far, we are still set to close tomorrow. This one will be called the Flatulent House. I hesitate to name it that, but it is all that comes to mind. The seller had a problem with passing gas as we talked at the house. I'm sure it was uncontrollable for him and I had a very, very hard time not changing facial expressions while talking to him as it happened. Whew.

Perp House

We closed on the house I mentioned getting under contract two weeks ago. This house was not where my wife found someone inside the house that had broken in, but is in the same neighborhood. This one will most likely be fixed and sold with owner financing. I will post the numbers and pictures within the coming week or two.

Audi House

We closed this morning on the Audi House. The seller had a nice Audi and honestly, that was the first thing that came to mind when trying to come up with a name for it. The house needs a lot of repairs and I will most likely wholesale it. Hopefully it will go quickly and profitably. Further details to come.

Next steps

- Find and hire a contractor.
- Move. That's it.

Week 29

Expanding Your Comfort Zone

This week, I really needed a break from the business, finishing the work on our house, and getting ready to move, so I decided to schedule a lesson on aerobatics with my flight instructor.

I went yesterday afternoon and had a blast! We went through the routine for the 2011 National Aerobatics Contest. I've flown aerobatics once before with my instructor in his Pitts S2B, but just to go through some of the basics. This time was all about learning and focusing on precision.

We worked on loops, rolls, going straight up and straight down, flying inverted, spinning and combinations thereof. It's very disorienting, to say the least, and took a lot of focus. The hardest part was handling the forces put on my body as we were pulling through some high Gs (high to me at least) — very difficult to stay focused and coordinated when your body feels like it weighs over 6 times what it does. I'd be lying if I said I was comfortable and confident throughout the lesson.

The reason I bring all of this up is that it gets into expanding my comfort zone. This lesson was not comfortable and was very challenging. Afterward, I wasn't elated; I was exhausted and wondering whether it is something I want to pursue. This questioning is normal in anything we do that takes us out of our comfort zone. After some more thought and looking back at the flight, I am again excited about it and know that I can push through the tough start and get comfortable doing it.

The same is true for beginning in flipping houses. It will be very uncomfortable in a lot of the things you will need to do. Working with

183

contractors, Realtors, buyers, sellers, other investors, etc., making low ball offers, worrying about whether you are making a good investment decision and so many other things. It will be uncomfortable, but it will eventually become second nature and you will succeed if only you push hard enough to work through it.

Please remember this. You must push through even though it feels like the biggest mountain you've ever climbed. Take it one step at a time and work through it.

Apart from flying, we put off moving for another week because we just had too much going on. My wife had called me while I was out and about and told me that she was stressing out about trying to move so soon. I myself was stressing and realized that we were just doing it to ourselves. There was not much a reason to do it so soon. Patience — don't we all need more of it?

My wife usually knows the best thing to do in a lot of situations. She tells me about these correct decisions and I file them away and do as I was doing, only to make mistakes and come back to her idea that then works. Of course, I have to then claim the idea as my own. Drives her crazy.

I finally found a good contractor and got our contract signed and he is starting work on the Honk Your Horn House on Monday. I found him at a house that was being rehabbed and I know he already works for two other investors but they are not keeping him busy. The thing that I liked most about him was that he was not trying to talk a big game. He didn't seem to feel the need to convince me of how good he is.

Despite that, I'm still looking for some more contractors to get bids and start work on the Perp House and the Front Yard Stink House. I've met some contractors and I'm awaiting their bids. Hopefully, I get another good one to start soon so I can then pick between that contractor and the one working on the Honk Your Horn House for the remaining rehabs.

Lead Analysis

Lead source	Number of leads
Buying website	13
Total	13

1. Tired of Getting Ripped Off
[Source: Website]

This homeowner wants to sell a 3 bedroom, 2 bath, 1000-square-foot house in a not-so-good neighborhood.

Here are the numbers:

- Asking Price: Make an offer
- Amount Owed: $5,000 (back taxes)
- Repairs: A lot (unconfirmed)
- After Repaired Value: $60,000
- Max Offer: $35,000 minus repairs

This house was vacant for a long time and somebody broke in and tore the place up and stole fixtures and other items. The sellers hired a contractor to fix it up and he just ran off with the money. Talk about a bad situation. These people are pretty motivated. I would go and contract this one for wholesale, but in the middle of this move, I decided to just bird-dog it.

2. Inherited and Just Want to Sell
[Source: Website]

A homeowner wants to sell a 2 bedroom, 2 bath, 1500-square-foot house in a good neighborhood.

Here are the numbers:

- Asking Price: $60,000
- Amount Owed: $0

- Repairs: Cosmetic (unconfirmed)
- After Repaired Value: $110,000
- Max Offer: $70,000 minus repairs

This seller inherited the house with his three other siblings. One lives in the house and is why I immediately asked if all were on board with wanting to sell. They are.

The neighborhood is a quaint, historic district with stone cottages. We used to live near here and know it well.

The house turned out to be a complete dump. The exterior stone walls are bulging out everywhere and the foundation is completely unlevel. This one would need about $40k in repairs and I am just not interested. They are getting five other offers, so I am going to wait and see if anyone bites. I have my doubts.

3. Buying New House
[Source: Website]

This homeowner wants to sell a 3 bedroom, 2 bath, 1500-square-foot house in a good neighborhood.

Here are the numbers:

- Asking Price: $63,000
- Amount Owed: $63,000
- Repairs: Cosmetic (about $12k based on photos)
- After Repaired Value: $95,000
- Max Offer: $50,000 ($62,000 - $12,000)

The seller called saying that he has a new house under contract and a loan approved, but needs to sell his old house. He is willing to sell for what is owed.

It turns out I had already analyzed this property. That is the nice thing about the lead manager software I developed (flippilot.com). With all of the leads we get, I wouldn't have remembered even coming across this one before.

It turns out that a wholesaler called me about this property last month. I knew I still couldn't make it work from the numbers and this allowed me to quickly move on to the next one. I did call another investor to try and bird-dog this one, though.

--

I got 10 other leads this week, but most were unmotivated sellers, which always makes for a bad deal on my end. One of the others was actually a commercial property that I passed on to another investor. Another owner called and wanted me to pay market value in cash—that is just asking the impossible, but I thought it was amusing.

Active deals

Flatulent House
We closed on the Flatulent House from last week. From contract to close was a little over 48 hours. The title company worked fast and got the commitment within a day. All was clear and it was easy. The name is a little crude, I know.

Next steps

- Move.
- Start marketing again.
- Get more contractors started and/or work at wholesaling some houses.

Week 30

You Must Act Fast

We got most of our stuff moved on Saturday. After years of drought, we ended up getting a lot of rain all weekend. We needed it, but we didn't. The move went as well as any move does. I haven't done that much physical labor in a long time and could feel it for days. I wanted to thank my friends and family for helping with the move. Our mentor showed up to see the house right after we arrived with the moving truck. He didn't know we would be unloading, but helped with the entire truckload without hesitation. It is great to have such wonderful family and friends!

Next time, we will be hiring movers. I say that every single move and we always end up doing it ourselves.

I put off returning some calls and emails while we were moving. All said and done, I know I missed out on one good deal and maybe two. I'm not going to beat myself up over it, but we all need to realize the opportunity cost when we try to save money by doing things ourselves.

I'll never forget one of the biggest rehabs we ever did. I'd had trouble scheduling contractors and ended up having a drywall crew scheduled to show up the next day without anyone to prep the studs throughout this giant house. There were nails everywhere and they needed to be removed. Not a big deal, but this was a huge house. I didn't know anyone I could hire to do the work on such short notice.

I ended up going over to the house to do the work myself. It was taking all day and I was very frustrated. Our mentor showed up and immediately gave me a lecture in a very irritated tone — no need to sugar coat it. I was missing out on deals that would make us thousands of dollars because I was busy swinging a hammer.

You have to realize where your time is best spent. This also gets into the good old 80/20 rule where 20 percent of the things you do produce 80 percent of the results. Work at focusing on those 20 percent.

The reason I hesitate to hire movers is that it seems packing and unpacking is where most of the time is spent anyway. Will I ever learn?

Despite being busy with the move, I did manage to find two more contractors. The first was a referral from a friend and the second was a referral from a Sherwin Williams store. I got several business cards off their wall there and also asked the sales rep if he recommended any of them. The manager recommended one, so I invited him to give a bid on the Flatulent House. He came in right at what I was figuring the job should cost. We just have to wait for the foundation to be leveled in the front and he can get started.

The other contractor is a painter that does tape, float, and texture as well. He did a small job for me at the new house and did excellent work, quickly and for a good price. I will have him do some work at our old house.

Although I'm currently working to get houses either sold or rehabbed and on the market, I will start shifting back to more marketing as the work is started on these houses.

Lead Analysis

Lead source	Number of leads
Yellow pages	3
Buying website	10
Drive for dollars	1
Wholesale	1
Total	**15**

1. Private Lender Foreclosure
[Source: Website]

A lender wants to sell a 3 bedroom, 1 bath, 1200-square-foot house in a so-so neighborhood.

Here are the numbers:

- Asking Price: Make an offer
- Amount Owed: $0
- Repairs: Quite a bit (unconfirmed)
- After Repaired Value: $60,000
- Max Offer: $35,000 minus repairs

This private lender foreclosed on someone that bought a house with owner financing. The lender was from out of town and just wanted to recoup his money. Unfortunately, I was too busy with the move this weekend to jump on this one as fast as I would have liked and another investor got it. I hate when that happens. This is why you need to do your best to visit houses as soon as possible; don't put it off.

2. Does Not Want to Commute So Far
[Source: Website]

This homeowner wants to sell a 3 bedroom, 2 bath, 1600-square-foot house in a good neighborhood.

Here are the numbers:

- Asking Price: $150,000
- Amount Owed: Unknown
- Repairs: Nothing (unconfirmed)
- After Repaired Value: $150,000
- Max Offer: $97,000 minus repairs

This seller lives pretty far outside of San Antonio in a retirement community and wants to sell to avoid her commute. I guess she is not yet retired.

She started in with how nice the house was and every little detail she thought set it apart. These are almost always a waste of time. I began to tell her that I would not be interested after she told me she wants what it has been listed for the last 3 months: $150k. It doesn't need repairs.

She kept mentioning that the house across the street sold for over $200k and that hers was nicer. I wonder why it hasn't sold yet, then. It's really as simple as that. Then came the, "It was appraised for X back in 2007." Do I need to even say anything here?

3. Tenants Tore Up
[Source: Website]

This homeowner wants to sell a 4 bedroom, 2.5 bath, 1400-square-foot house in a decent neighborhood.

Here are the numbers:

- Asking Price: $73,000
- Amount Owed: Would not say
- Repairs: A lot (unconfirmed)
- After Repaired Value: $90,000
- Max Offer: $58,000 minus repairs

The seller had tenants in the house that completely destroyed it. She does not have the financing or patience to fix it back up and rent it out again. This one is near the Flatulent House and I knew I would want this one for around the same price as that one, so I gave her a ballpark figure of $45k. I did this because she would not tell me how much she owed and just didn't seem like her motivation level was where it needed to be. She immediately told me that wouldn't work.

--

The other 12 leads this week didn't get anywhere for a variety of reasons. Some owed too much, others were in bad neighborhoods, and others just were not motivated enough to make a deal with. I did manage to bird-dog a few, though.

Active deals

Audi House

The Audi House needed more work than I wanted to tackle right now with how many houses we have in inventory. An investor friend of mine was looking for another project and expressed interest in this house. He looked at it very quickly and met me to sign a contract at my asking price. This should be a quick wholesale. I will post the numbers after it closes in a couple of weeks.

Def Leppard House

It's been a while since I last mentioned this one, but I've had the Def Leppard House under contract for a couple of weeks. The inspection has been done and minor repairs have been made. The only things they wanted fixed were a running toilet, the stinky garage, and a couple doors that had phantom swings. They also wanted the AC serviced. We should be closing this sale within a couple of weeks.

Perp House

We checked on the Perp House yesterday to make sure all was well while it was sitting there waiting for me to get to it. The house was fine, but there was a strong smell coming from the hall bathroom. Immediately, I knew where it was coming from and I hesitatingly lifted the lid to the toilet. Yep, just as I suspected: full of everything and very disgusting. I turned the water on to the toilet and gave it a flush (with the lid down, because I did not want to deal with any suspense induced with watching the nasty water slowly rise to the brim. I'm getting shivers just thinking about it while typing this.

It did not overflow, thank God. I then flushed again for good measure and thought all was well. Just to check, I lifted the lid again and noticed the water swirling around at the top of the bowl. Everything still there and the smell spewing even more strongly because of the disturbance. Gross.

I called up my trusty old contractor that we were having problems with — old habits die hard. He immediately showed up, grabbed the plunger and went to town. This guy was crazy. The sewage water was splashing everywhere and he was just ramming that plunger in there without any concern for the water splashing out and very near to him. I was standing a good ten feet away mainly because the wall of stink held me back. Oh, the joys of rehabs and what others leave for the new owner. Not my idea of a good housewarming gift.

Next steps

- Finish moving.
- Mail some postcards.
- Get contractors started and work at wholesaling some houses.

Week 31

Time to Wholesale

We currently have three rehabs in progress and still need to have a contractor do minor touch-ups at our old house to get it on the market. Three at one time is really my limit. If they are light rehabs, which these are, it is manageable. Right now, rehabs are taking place at the Honk Your Horn House, the Perp House and the Flatulent House. The Front Yard Stink house is still awaiting rehab.

I mailed follow-up postcards to 178 addresses, which were ones we found while driving for dollars months ago that have already had several letters and postcards mailed to them.

The leads have slowed quite a bit due to my time spent on focusing on rehabs. If I am going to be wholesaling more, I will need to ramp the marketing back up.

We are still unpacking and getting settled at our new house and all of this going on at once has made us really busy. My son is due in December and I don't want to be in the middle of a ton of rehabs and other projects, so I am probably going to be doing more wholesaling as deals come up. Quick cash is always awesome and I am looking forward to working the business a little differently.

Lead Analysis

Lead source	Number of leads
Yellow pages	1
Buying website	7
Referral	1
Total	**9**

1. Lake House Without a View
[Source: Website]

A homeowner wants to sell a 3 bedroom, 2 bath, 1700-square-foot house in a good neighborhood.

Here are the numbers:

- Asking Price: $45,000
- Amount Owed: $0
- Repairs: Trashed (unconfirmed)
- After Repaired Value: Unknown
- Max Offer: Unknown minus repairs

This homeowner lives out of town. They had started building this house years ago and then had to move. After moving, they decided to rent the house. (I guess it was in livable condition if not complete). The tenants have since moved out, but only after trashing the place. This seller is motivated and wants to sell pronto.

The house is on a 2+ acre lot and the seller owns the 1+ acre lot next to it. She is including both with the sale. My father went out to see this one because I was wrapped up with some things. I wanted to move fast and he helped by taking a look for me.

The driveway at the house had been completely washed out by the hard rains we got here a couple of weeks ago. The house was built by the homeowners — not contracted to be built, but actually built by their hand.

The foundation was all wrong and it just got worse from there. Even with the acreage, the place was not worth the hassle at almost any price.

The best bet for this one was to bird-dog it and try to make a quick referral fee instead. Unfortunately, none of my investors wanted it, either. You would think at that price it would be a good deal, but there are some surprising things out there.

2. Big Improvements Made
[Source: Website]

This homeowner wants to sell a 2 bedroom, 3 bath, 2700-square-foot house in a good area.

Here are the numbers:

- Asking Price: $368,500
- Amount Owed: $265,000
- Repairs: Master remodel (unconfirmed)
- After Repaired Value: $250,000
- Max Offer: $162,000 minus repairs

The sellers are relocating, so they want to sell. They mentioned having done a big improvement to the outside, including an organic garden, landscaping, several garden shades convertible for greenhouses, a rainwater collection system and additional outbuildings.

It sounds nice — and pricey. I think this may be a case where homeowners put a lot of money into improvements for a property and expect to get 100% and then some back on what they spent. It just doesn't work that way. Next.

3. Mother-In-Law's Condo
[Source: Yellow Pages]

The homeowner wants to sell a 2 bedroom, 2 bath, 2000-square-foot condo in a decent neighborhood.

Here are the numbers:

- Asking Price: Make an offer
- Amount Owed: $0
- Repairs: Cosmetic (unconfirmed)
- After Repaired Value: $80,000
- Max Offer: $50,000 minus repairs

This guy was selling his mother-in-law's condo as she does not live there anymore. He is from Mexico and will not be here long. The comparable sales are all over the place for the condos near this one. They go from the 50's to 90's and it is pretty hard to get a solid idea. The seller believes this one is larger than the rest and does not need much in repairs.

I am putting an ARV of 80k on this one and may adjust if I see it. I made a ballpark offer to see where they are at on this one being that they have no idea what to ask for it. No luck.

--

The other 6 leads this week were mostly owners who owe too much. I was able to bird-dog two in a bad neighborhood, though.

Active deals

Perp House
I was considering wholesaling the Perp House, but decided to fix it up and sell it with owner financing instead. The work and materials will cost $4,000. We will also need to pay for new carpet throughout as well. This is well below the estimated budget of $10,000 so, if we have any surprises we will still be within our budget. Updates are forthcoming and deal details can be found in the Flipped Houses section.

The Flatulent House
This one is in the process of being rehabbed and will be listed with our Realtor when completed.

Our new contractor has agreed to do the work with materials for $5,500. We still need to pay for carpeting throughout most of the house and some AC repair work and landscaping. Also, the new garage doors are not a part of this bid and will be extra. These additional costs will likely make up the difference in our budget for this house. Further details can be found in Flipped Houses, and I'll continue to update progress on this house in the coming weeks.

Def Leppard
The Def Leppard House is set to close tomorrow. Profit from this one is looking to be pretty good. Details are available at the end of the book.

Rambo House
This one is one that I had looked at a couple of weeks ago. I had to offer lower than what they owed. The husband had a job transfer out of state and was already there. The wife wanted to move and join him, but needed to deal with the house first. They were hoping to make $20k or more over what they owed, but opted for a quick sale instead.

We ended up agreeing that I'd pay what they owed, which was my MAO. This one will be wholesaled. Final details of the sale will be in the Flipped Houses section.

Next steps
- Finish unpacking.
- Mail some more postcards.
- Manage rehabs.
- Move staging furniture from the Def Leppard House to the Honk Your Horn House.

Week 32

Another Flip Complete

This week, I got 100 more probate leads and will be mailing letters to them this week. Our family friend that is doing the letters is also preparing a repeat mailing for the addresses we already had.

If I find myself twiddling my thumbs this week, I will put together another absentee owner mailing. I need to get the leads coming in again in force. Things have slowed a little with our preoccupation with the move.

I made a couple offers this week but they don't seem very promising. Time was spent focusing on the rehabs and still getting settled at the new house. My mind keeps wanting to start focusing on more marketing and I need to find the right balance. It can be difficult to rehab 3-4 properties and keep the marketing going.

Lead Analysis

Lead source	Number of leads
Yellow pages	1
Buying website	5
Referral	1
Total	**7**

1. Outgrown House
[Source: Website]

A homeowner wants to sell a 3 bedroom, 2 bath, 1200-square-foot house in a so-so neighborhood.

Here are the numbers:

- Asking Price: $89,000
- Amount Owed: $126,000
- Repairs: Cosmetic (unconfirmed)
- After Repaired Value: $80,000
- Max Offer: $50,000 minus repairs

This situation is a tough one. The neighborhood has been hit hard by foreclosures and values have dropped significantly. These houses are only 5 years old. From this example, you can see what happens when you look at what is owed versus the current ARV. Ouch.

2. Divorce
[Source: Website]

This homeowner wants to sell a 3 bedroom, 1 bath, 1000-square-foot house in a good neighborhood.

Here are the numbers:

- Asking Price: $89,000
- Amount Owed: $0
- Repairs: $6,000 (cosmetic)
- After Repaired Value: $90,000
- Max Offer: $52,000 ($58,000 - $6,000)

The owners are getting divorced and need to sell this house. They owe nothing, but are asking what it is worth. I went to see this house and made an offer of $50,000. They are considering it, but they didn't seem real thrilled.

3. Facing Foreclosure
[Source: Yellow Pages]

The homeowner wants to sell a 2 bedroom, 1 bath, 900-square-foot house in a bad neighborhood.

Here are the numbers:

- Asking Price: Make an offer
- Amount Owed: $6,000
- Repairs: A lot (unconfirmed)
- After Repaired Value: $50,000
- Max Offer: $25,000 minus repairs

These sellers sounded very motivated, but did not tell me everything that is owed. This area is rough and I am just not interested. I passed it on to a buddy.

--

This week, I got 4 other leads, but all owed too much or were in bad areas. I bird-dogged two and wished the others well.

Active deals

Def Leppard House
We just closed on the sale of this house. A full timeline for this deal, as well as final numbers are at the end of the book.

Audi House
Since I decided to wholesale it, we just closed on this one. The first person to see it bought it in cash, as-is. It worked out great. Numbers and other details are available in the Flipped Houses section.

Other Properties
The rehabs at the Honk Your Horn House, the Perp House and the Flatulent House are going well. The Flatulent House got its garage converted back from a den. It now has a two-car garage again. We can't stand garage conversions. Some people like the extra space, but I think most people (especially the guys) would rather have the garage. The new contractors have been great so far and have done everything as agreed.

Next steps

- Get some probate letters out.
- Mail some more postcards.
- Manage our existing rehabs.
- Work at wholesaling a couple of houses.
- Follow up on old leads.

Week 33

Another Wholesale Flipped

This week, I went to fly a couple of really cool older airplanes at a grass airstrip south of town. Just as I was a couple minutes from the field, I noticed a giant buck running out of a field toward the road. He was running *fast*!

I was doing about 55 or 60 and it seemed as though he was keeping up. (I'm sure he wasn't but it looked that way at the time). My instinct was to hit the brakes, but I realized that I would probably beat the dear to our intersection, so I kept going. As I passed, I saw him leap up and over the back end of my car. I watched him fall and slide on his hind end a little as he lost his footing. He didn't even wait a millisecond to transition from the slide back into a 50+ mph run. We were both very lucky to have missed each other.

Apart from that, I spent some time this week calling the follow-up reminders that were due. I had a lot as we've been so busy. For some of them, I was checking the county appraisal website first to see if a new deed had been recorded, signaling that they had sold the property. One of the ones I was really interested in showed a transaction, which was disappointing — but not quite as much as when found out that they just painted the place and have it under contract after 6 days on the market. Darn.

This goes to show why it is so important to use the follow-up system and constantly follow up on old leads. You'd better believe that it put me back in follow-up mode.

I didn't have much time to put together any new mailings but fully intend to this coming week. The letters for the probate leads we got last week should be going out as well. We need to generate more leads — that's all it really takes.

Lead Analysis

Lead source	Number of leads
Yellow pages	1
Buying website	11
Total	**12**

1. Investment Property Wants to Cash Out Of
[Source: Website]

The homeowner wants to sell a 3 bedroom, 2 bath, 1200-square-foot house in a decent neighborhood.

Here are the numbers:

- Asking Price: $70,000
- Amount Owed: $0
- Repairs: Central air & cosmetic (unconfirmed)
- After Repaired Value: $80,000
- Max Offer: $50,000 minus repairs

The seller bought this HUD house a year ago and now wants to sell. He doesn't seem to be interested in getting much less than what it is worth, though. The problem with the house is that it does not have central air conditioning and the pitch of the roof is such that it would be impossible to run ductwork through the attic. It would still sell without the central air, just at a lower price. I made him a ballpark offer.

2. Lost Job then Got a New, Lower Paying Job
[Source: Website]

A homeowner wants to sell this 4 bedroom, 2.5 bath, 3300-square-foot house in a good neighborhood.

Here are the numbers:

- Asking Price: $180,000
- Amount Owed: $180,000
- Repairs: Cosmetic and plumbing (unconfirmed)
- After Repaired Value: $180,000
- Max Offer: $120,000 minus repairs

This homeowner lost his job at the beginning of the year. He ended up having to take a lower paying job and now can't afford the house they are living in. He mentioned low flow to several fixtures in the house and is not sure what is causing it.

They owe what it is worth but wanted an offer from me anyway, so I made them a ballpark offer based on my usual calculation. He didn't immediately get angry, so that was a good sign. He said he would have to talk it over with his wife.

3. Weird Complex
[Source: Website]

This owner wants to sell their five one-bedroom apartments with a restaurant in front.

Here are the numbers:

- Asking Price: $120,000
- Amount Owed: Nothing
- Repairs: Everything (unconfirmed)
- After Repaired Value: Unknown
- Max Offer: FREE

The owner's health has diminished and she needs to sell this property because the city is going to tear it down. The picture of it on Google Maps was enough for me to end the conversation early. Wow. It's horrible and I can see why the city wants it gone. The place is vacant and the seller had plenty of time to comply with the city but has not and it will now be the new owner's problem. Not an impossible task, but a very time-consuming one. I may have had some interest, but not anywhere near the price she is expecting.

--

I managed to pass along 4 of the 9 other leads I got. The others just didn't have the numbers to work.

Active deals

Audi House
The Audi House has been sold as-is and I couldn't be happier. Less work for me and some quick cash in our pocket. My intentions were to rehab and sell this house, but I just got too busy and I couldn't resist when the first investor to see it wanted it.

Bought it - check. Didn't do any work to it - check. Sold it cash - check. Got a check - check. You can never have too many checks.

There was no high-dollar crazy check picture on this one because we received a huge loan overage at the closing when we bought it because I had intended to rehab it. We actually had to bring money to the table to close it when we sold. It's really sort of weird paying money at closing when selling a house considering what we ended up making on this wholesale.

More details on this sale can be found in the Flipped Houses section at the end of the book.

Flatulent House & Honk Your Horn
These rehabs are almost complete. We should be putting in flooring, cleaning and hopefully staging both next week.

Perp House
The Perp House is complete and up for sale with owner financing. Final deal details can be found in Flipped Houses.

Next week

- Mail some more postcards.
- Manage rehabs.
- Work at wholesaling a house I have under contract.
- Follow up on old leads.

Week 34

Another Awesome Wholesale

As you know, I had two new crews working at the rehabs over the last several weeks. One contractor was very professional and I did not have any problems with him. His work was great and he was on time. The extras did not cost a fortune and some minor extras were just done for free. This is what you want. The other guy...*arrgh*!

I don't know how many times he told me he was finished. The house is about 45 minutes away from where I now live, so it really was wasting my time every time I went out there. I don't think I've ever had to write that many punch lists. The items that needed to be fixed or that were just not done were even plastered with blue tape so that they could walk through the house and know where things needed attention. After the first round, they removed some of the tape and did not do the work. It's hard to keep a level head at this point. Trust me, he knew I was not happy. I'll just leave it at that.

Can you guess who is going to get the next job? The problem contractor because he keeps things interesting. Just kidding, of course.

I also had my guy put out 40 bandit signs. I wanted to get the phone ringing right away, so I had him put them up on Tuesday. Not a good idea.

He called me and was frantically telling me that code compliance stopped him and hassled him for a long time. They then made him drive back down the really long and busy street to pull the signs he just posted off the poles. They followed him and watched him take them down. He left some on the side streets and I got a couple calls from those, so it wasn't a complete waste of money.

They are *really* cracking down on those things these days. Part of me is wondering about this whole situation, though, since the code compliance office didn't call the number on the signs.

Overall, leads picked up quite a bit this week. With the rehabs pretty much completed, I can focus more on the marketing and flying. Did I say flying? I meant working on the business…

Leads Analyzed

Lead source	Number of leads
Bandit signs	2
Yellow pages	2
Buying website	13
Wholesale	1
REO	1
Referral	1
Total	**20**

1. Slab Leak Likely
[Source: Website]

A homeowner wants to sell a 3 bedroom, 1 bath, 1000-square-foot house in a not-so-good neighborhood.

Here are the numbers:

- Asking Price: $47,000
- Amount Owed: $47,000
- Repairs: Slab leak and cosmetic (unconfirmed)
- After Repaired Value: $55,000
- Max Offer: $30,000 minus repairs

This seller has the misfortune of most likely having a slab leak and the resulting serious foundation problems. These houses are no joke and usually require a lot of costly repairs. Too much is owed to even consider, anyway. I don't want to have anything to do with this house.

2. Rehabbed and Needs Out
[Source: Website]

The homeowner wants to sell a 3 bedroom, 2 bath, 1200-square-foot house outside of town.

Here are the numbers:

- Asking Price: $160,000
- Amount Owed: $115,000
- Repairs: None (unconfirmed)
- After Repaired Value: $100,000
- Max Offer: $65,000 minus repairs

The seller rehabbed this house and had it sold once but the buyers backed out. The MLS did not show any listing changes to reflect it being under contract at any time. His idea of the value is super skewed and way too high. I'm not remotely interested.

3. Cannot Afford Anymore
[Source: Website]

A homeowner wants to sell a 4 bedroom, 2.5 bath, 2000-square-foot house in a so-so neighborhood.

Here are the numbers:

- Asking Price: $80,000
- Amount Owed: $61,000
- Repairs: Kitchen and in-ground pool repair (unconfirmed)
- After Repaired Value: $90,000
- Max Offer: $59,000 minus repairs

They cannot afford to keep the house anymore and are having trouble keeping up with the repairs. Though they are asking $80k, I'm sure they will be willing to take a lot closer to what they owe. I would still need it cheaper, so I just bird-dogged it.

4. Realtor Selling Run-Down Old House
[Source: Bandit Signs]

The homeowner wants to sell a 5 bedroom, 1 bath, 2000-square-foot house in a decent neighborhood.

Here are the numbers:

- Asking Price: $105,000
- Amount Owed: $0
- Repairs: Everything (unconfirmed)
- After Repaired Value: $150,000
- Max Offer: $90,000 minus repairs

This house needs everything. The rehab costs for these old houses can get out of hand very quickly and I would rather avoid them. Five deals can be done while you are working on one of these. I will be following up to see if I can get it cheap enough to wholesale, though.

--

The other 16 leads from this week didn't pan out. The majority simply owed too much, so I couldn't do anything to help them. There was also a mix of bad neighborhoods and tiny houses, which I bird-dogged. I made offers on a few others, but the sellers weren't interested.

Active deals

Front Yard Stink House
The Front Yard Stink House was wholesaled. My intentions were to fix it and sell it with owner financing, but with four rehabs going, it was just

sitting and waiting for work to be done. I stuck a sign in the front yard and put an ad in the paper to sell it as-is for cash.

It didn't take long to sell (maybe three days). The price I had on it was $55,000 for a cash, as-is sale. I only had to show it twice. The second family I showed it to wanted it. They are going to fix it up and live in it. It's an interesting story really.

They called to inquire about the house and I quickly wanted to make sure they understood that the price was for *cash* and that I would need to see a bank statement or other proof of funds before signing a contract. They said they couldn't do that because it wasn't in a bank. I asked where it was and she told me they had the actual cash.

This was a first for me. They saw the house and talked it over for about ten minutes while I sat in my car. Their decision had been made — they wanted it and were willing to close in three days We went to a restaurant and signed the contract.

After signing, I asked if they had won the lottery. The husband then informed me that he had been shot. He works as a security guard, but was not on duty. One day, he went to visit his brother who works at a pawn shop and his wife and daughter came with him. While at the shop, a robber entered the store and was ordering everyone to the floor. The guy's daughter was very scared and just froze. He wasn't about to allow this scum to point a gun at his daughter, so he pulled his piece and opened up on the guy. He fired 8 times at the robber and hit him 5 times. The robber hit the guy once, but he was still of the right mind to run to the front door to make sure the robber didn't have backup that would come and try to help him, then held him down until the police came.

The pawn shop settled with him for his pain and suffering.

What a hero. This was the best buyer I've ever had. There was a slight issue with the fact that most title companies will not accept actual cash as they require a cashier's check or wire. In the end, the buyers ended up opening a bank account and getting a cashier's check.

Find the numbers and timeline for this sale in the Flipped Houses section at the end of the book.

Perp House
We got a call from a buyer wanting to see the Perp House. After seeing it, they decided they wanted it. Not bad for a first showing. Their credit, income and job history were great. All looks good and we will be closing within a couple of weeks. Numbers will be listed in the Flipped Houses section, which starts on the next page.

Next steps

- Mail some more postcards.
- Have three rehabbed houses on the market and listed.
- Work at wholesaling a house that I have under contract.
- Follow up on old leads.

Flipped Houses

Sad to say it, but that concludes the 34 weeks of *Flipping Houses Exposed*. Life was just about to get a lot more hectic with the birth of my son, Weston. I didn't want to be super busy with too many things going on, so I did take it easy for a while afterward.

It's incredible to have a life where it's possible to switch gears and take it easy when we want to. Those sleepless nights with the new baby were not so bad because I didn't have to conquer the world each morning. This is the reason I wanted to share all of this information in the first place.

There is a big hill to climb when you get started flipping houses and I wanted to show you that hill. I wanted to show you that it's surmountable and that things do pick up and get easier. So many people give up because they don't truly believe that getting deals is really possible for them.

It took me several months to start pulling in deals during these past 34 weeks, and I was doing a lot of marketing, but I'm sure you noticed that after a while it seemed like I was putting another one under contract every week. This is the snowball effect — as you start marketing, leads come in, then you nurture those leads and continue doing marketing until all of a sudden, you've got *too many* houses to manage! You've got to start with a small one though. Start with those baby steps and you will eventually be running — hopefully not away from a perp at one of your houses!

To sum up this experience, you'll find the details of each deal we made in the 34 weeks. Some of these did sell and close *after* the 34 weeks had passed, but these were all properties purchased as the result of my marketing efforts and negotiating during these weeks.

In addition to financial details, you'll find timelines and scope of work for the rehabbed properties, as well as links to before and after photos.

Hidden Iron House

This one was a lead we got in Week 1, and then closed on in Week 5. It was a 2 bedroom, 1 bath with a 1.5 car garage; 907-square-foot house built in 1995. This seller was asking a reasonable price from the beginning and accepted my offer just a few hours after I made it. Note: We would have closed sooner had we not had the problem with the FHA 90 day flipping rule.

Timeline
- Purchase date: April 18, 2011
- Listing date: May 5, 2011
- Contract date: June 16, 2011
- Closing date: July 18, 2011
- Total days from purchase to resell: 92 days

Scope of Work
Exterior
- Replace rotted exterior wood
- Install new light fixtures in front and back, new door, and replace mailbox
- Scrape, caulk and paint exterior trim and garage door
- Repair fence (replace any rotted and extremely warped boards and fix post in back)
- Interior
- Remove carpet, blinds, curtains throughout
- Install new vinyl stick tile in kitchen, pantry, entry, utility and bathroom
- Replace rotted baseboards
- Clean and secure air registers
- Replace doors and door trim where necessary and install door stops
- Install new vanity light and faucet and replace light bulbs where needed
- Remove medicine cabinet and install mirror

- Make sure all switch and plug plates match throughout the house. Replace broken ones.
- Install new toilet seats
- Repair minor electrical in attic
- Install new chandelier in dining room
- Professional painting throughout
- Smoke detectors where necessary

Numbers

Initial Costs and Assumptions
- Purchase price: $25,000
- Settlement fees: $1,400 (title policy, closing fee, insurance, loan fee)
- Estimated repairs: $8,000 (estimated $10k, but I think we can do it cheaper)
- Estimated resale price: $70,000
- Estimated profit: $35,600 minus holding costs and selling costs

Actual Costs
- Holding costs (mortgage interest, property taxes, insurance): $1,560.74
- Realtor commission: $3,912.70
- Buyer cost assistance: $4,268.40
- Title policy & survey: $951.35
- Other costs: $357.95

Final Numbers
- Repairs: $8,157.44
- Total closing costs: $9,490.40 (OUCH!)
- Actual resale price: $71,140
- Actual profit: $25,531.42

You can see photos of this house at
http://flippingjunkie.com/hidden-iron-house/

Def Leppard House

This was a 4 bedroom, 3.5 bathroom, 2500-square-foot house that was built in 2006. This was a lead from Week 10 that we got under contract in Week 12. In this case, the seller originally wanted around $150k and when I offered $95k, she didn't seem interested. Later, when I followed up, we agreed to a $100k price.

Timeline
- Purchase date: June 13, 2011
- Listing date: July 21, 2011
- Contract date: September 26, 2011
- Closing date: October 21, 2011
- Total days from purchase to resell: 130

Scope of Work
Exterior
- Wash and paint exterior where necessary
- Install new back door and new door hardware and kick plate in front
- Clean windows and columns
- Install new doorbell
- Minor landscaping

Interior
- Remove damaged blinds from the breakfast room
- Patch cracks and imperfections in walls and ceilings
- Install light bulbs where needed throughout
- Make sure all switch and plug plates match throughout the house
- Minor electrical
- Install new ceiling fans in living room and upstairs den
- Replace light fixture at top of stairs
- Re-caulk around toilets and where necessary
- Spray garage to remove pet odor

- Professional painting
- Clean return air vent and opening and install new air filter
- Install door stops and smoke detectors where necessary

Numbers

Initial Costs and Assumptions
- Purchase price: $100,000
- Settlement fees: $2,159 (title policy, closing fee, insurance, loan fee)
- Estimated repairs: $6,500
- Resale price: $170,000 (might have to go down to $160k quickly)
- Estimated profit: $63,841

Actual Costs
- Holding costs: $7,778.36 (HOA fees, mortgage interest, taxes, insurance)
- Realtor commissions: $9,069.50
- Buyer cost assistance: $5,874.10
- Title policy & home warranty: $1,685
- Other costs: $447.95

Final Numbers
- Repairs: $6,758.90
- Total closing costs: $17,076.55 (OUCH!)
- Actual resale price: $164,900
- Actual Profit: $31,127.19

Before photos and details: http://flippingjunkie.com/def-leppard-house/

After photos:
http://flippingjunkie.com/def-leppard-house-for-sale-after-pictures/

Historic House

This was a 4 bedroom, 2 bath, 2700-square-foot house built in 1939. The house has a detached garage and mother-in-law suite that is a decent size. There is an in-ground pool and still plenty of space in the backyard.

As this was a wholesale, it was bought and sold quickly. We originally got the lead on this house in Week 8 and finally closed in Week 15 after delays with the bank. It was officially wholesaled a few days later.

Timeline
- Purchase date: June 28, 2011
- Resale date: July 15, 2011

Numbers
- Purchase price: $95,000
- Settlement fees (buy side): $2,588 (title policy, closing fee, insurance, loan fee)
- Resale price: $150,000
- Settlement fees (sell side): $1,600 (closing fee, half of the title policy, taxes, loan interest)
- Profit: $50,812

The ARV for this house is about $300,000. I estimated the repairs at about $60k if you watched your expenditures closely. We did not do a single thing to this house with the exception of dumping a ton of shock into the pool to keep it from becoming a swamp.

There have been several occasions in the past where we could have sold a house quickly for a decent cash price, as-is, and opted to fix it and sell for more of a profit. Inevitably, we ended up making less than we would have had we just sold to the cash buyer. Take this to heart, especially in this market.

Since this was a wholesale, rather than a rehab, I just have this one photo: http://www.flippingjunkie.com/media/images/houses/HistoricHouse Wholesale.jpg

Frustration House

This is a 3 bedroom, 2.5 bathroom, 2300-square-foot house that was built in 2001. This lead came in about six months before I started blogging about my flipping experience, but the seller called back in Week 14. We got it under contract in Week 16 and finally sold it a few months after finishing the blog series.

Timeline
- Purchase date: July 20, 2011
- Listing date: September 2, 2011
- Contract date: January 24, 2012
- Closing date: March 6, 2012
- Total days from purchase to resell: 230 days (7 1/2 months)

This one took a while to sell. I attribute it to the fact that we didn't do much to update the kitchen and master bath.

Scope of Work
Exterior
- Power wash, paint and repair exterior where necessary
- Replace warped deck rail
- Install new doorknobs and deadbolts for the front door, back door and door to the garage.
- Install new light fixtures for front and back porch
- Clean windows and install new screens

Interior
- Minor repairs on walls and ceilings
- Professional painting
- Tighten fridge water connection and paint handle on fridge with correct paint
- Replace garbage disposal
- Repair kitchen cabinets
- Hook up automatic garage door opener

223

- Replace light fixtures, doorknobs, lightbulbs, switch plates, door stops
- Replace all mini-blinds
- Re-caulk around toilets and where necessary
- Clean return air vent and opening and install new air filter
- Install smoke detectors where necessary
- Repair broken cabinet door in bathroom
- Replace both faucets in bathrooms
- Remove carpet and install vinyl stick down tile
- Replace one light fixture

Numbers

Initial Costs and Assumptions
- Purchase price: $105,000
- Settlement fees: $2,486 (title policy, closing fee, insurance, loan fee)
- Estimated repairs: $8,000
- Resale price: $175,000
- Estimated profit: $59,514 minus holding costs and selling costs (estimating about 17k)

Actual costs
- Holding costs: $11,376.22 (HOA, interest, taxes, insurance, utilities)
- Realtor commissions: $12,020.00
- Buyer cost assistance: $2,880.55
- Title policy & home warranty: $1,536.95
- Other costs: $87.00

Final Numbers
- Repairs: $10,232.31
- Total closing costs: $16,524.50 (OUCH!)
- Actual resale price: $164,000
- Actual profit: $18,380.97

If you aren't paying attention, you can easily go into the red and lose money on a deal. Once we realized how long it had been on the market, we had to start dropping the price and even gave a $3,000 bonus to the buyer's agent. Sometimes you just have to stop the bleeding.

Photos: http://www.flippingjunkie.com/2011/the-frustration-house

Flatulent House

This was a 3 bedroom, 2 bath, 1700-square-foot house built in 1981. I had this analyzed before I started blogging my journey, and got in under contract in Week 28. The Flatulent House sold in a reasonable amount of time.

Timeline
- Purchase date: September 30, 2011
- Listing date: November 23, 2011
- Contract date: December 21, 2011
- Closing date: February 3, 2012
- Total days from purchase to resell: 126 days (4 months)

Scope of Work
Exterior
- Replace rotted siding
- Convert the "converted garage" back into a garage
- Paint entire exterior
- Install new exterior light fixtures

Interior
- Remove carpet throughout
- Remove wallpaper and trim
- Install bi-fold doors in one bedroom closet and install wire shelf
- Patch and texture cracks and imperfections in walls and ceilings
- Professional painting
- Rehab kitchen cabinets and install new hardware

- Replace dishwasher
- Tile kitchen and breakfast area
- Replace light fixtures
- Remove window treatments
- Re-caulk around toilets and where necessary
- Install smoke detectors and door stops where necessary
- Tile floor in hall bath
- Replace vanity, mirror, faucet, shower head, towel rack, toilet seat, vanity light in hall bath and master bath
- Rehab cabinets in master bath
- Tile toilet and vanity area

Numbers

Initial Costs and Assumptions
- Purchase price: $48,500
- Settlement fees: $1,258 (doc fees, closing fee, insurance)
- Estimated repairs: $10,000
- Resale price: $90,000
- Estimated holding/selling costs: $9,000
- Estimated profit: $21,242

Actual costs
- Holding costs: $3,180.58 (interest, taxes, insurance, utilities)
- Realtor commissions: $5,250.00
- Buyer cost assistance: $1,750.00
- Title policy & home warranty: $761.00
- Other costs: $540.45

Final numbers
- Repairs: $12,652.17
- Total closing costs: $8,301.45
- Actual resale price: $87,500
- Actual profit: $13,607.80

The actual profit was not quite what was estimated, but is it ever? The money sure does smell good though.

Before photos: http://www.flippingjunkie.com/2011/flatulent-house

After photos: http://www.flippingjunkie.com/flatulent-house-after-pictures

Honk Your Horn House

This was a 4 bedroom, 2 bath, 1500-square-foot house in a good neighborhood. This was the one where the seller's grandson was honking the horn as we signed the contract, hence the name. This lead came in Week 23 and was sold after I finished recording my journey online.

After it was finally on the market, it sold in a reasonable amount of time as well. With it being for sale over the holidays, it's understandable.

Timeline
- Purchase date: September 8, 2011
- Listing date: November 23, 2011
- Contract date: January 23, 2012
- Closing date: February 17, 2012
- Total days from purchase to resell: 162 days (5 months)

Scope of Work
Exterior
- Replace rotted siding and install trim
- Install new doorknobs and deadbolts for back door and door to garage
- Install new light fixture for back porch
- Paint entire exterior
- Replace fencing where rotted or missing

Interior
- Remove carpet and wallpaper borders throughout
- Replace front door frame and repair door

227

- Texture any imperfections in walls and ceilings, remove stickers, and repair sheetrock
- Professional painting
- Rehab kitchen cabinets and install new hardware
- Replace kitchen faucet
- Replace light fixtures
- Replace interior doors
- Replace interior doorknobs and strike plates
- Remove all mini-blinds
- Re-caulk around toilets and where necessary
- Replace return air grill and install new air filter
- Install smoke detectors where necessary
- Replace all door stops

Master Bath and Hall Bath
- Remove everything except the toilet
- Repair walls and texture
- Tile floors
- Install new tub, tile surround and trim kit
- Install new vanity, faucet, light and towel rack
- Install new mirror

Numbers
Initial Costs and Assumptions
- Purchase price: $65,000
- Settlement fees: $3,379 (title policy, closing fee, insurance, loan fee)
- Estimated repairs: $15,000
- Resale price: $120,000
- Estimated holding/selling costs: $12,000
- Estimated profit: $24,621

Actual costs
- Holding costs: $7,716.67 (interest, taxes, insurance, utilities)
- Realtor commissions: $6,380.00
- Buyer cost assistance: $4,640.00
- Other costs: $2,440.92

Final Numbers
- Repairs: $18,559.65
- Total closing costs: $13,460.92
- Actual resale price: $116,000
- Actual profit: $7,883.76

That's not quite the number a TV show would tell ya, is it? This is why they don't like to show the real costs. Another example of how holding and closing costs can eat your lunch (over several decades, that's a lot of lunches).

These were not really representative of our typical profits, but do show the reality of what happens when rehab budgets get busted, closing costs balloon and holding costs escalate.

Before photos:
http://www.flippingjunkie.com/2011/honk-your-horn-house

After photos:
http://www.flippingjunkie.com/honk-your-horn-after-pictures

Perp House

This was a 3 bedroom, 1 bath, 1100-square-foot house in a so-so neighborhood. The lead came in Week 26 and we had in under contract to be sold by Week 34.

The Perp House was sold with owner financing. The buyer now makes payments to us instead of getting a bank loan to buy the house. We do these from time to time for retirement purposes. They are much better than rentals as the buyer is responsible for taxes, insurance, maintenance, and everything else. We just have to make sure they always have insurance and pay the property taxes every year.

House Flip Timeline

- Purchase date: September 26, 2011
- For Sale date: November 3, 2011
- Contract date: November 22, 2011
- Closing date: November 29, 2011
- Total days from purchase to resell: 64 days (2 months)

Scope of Work

Exterior

- Haul off fallen branch
- Remove copper line from front and side
- Add base and dirt to backyard by the garage door
- Power wash siding
- Hook up dryer vent
- Clean out garage and shed

Interior

- Remove carpet throughout
- Install ceiling fan
- Repair cracks in walls and ceiling
- Clean and re-caulk shower tub and toilets
- Replace knobs on dresser in master
- Replace blinds
- Install door and doorknob
- Replace hall light
- Prime and paint all paneling and doors
- Frame out the mirror with trim in master
- Touch up kitchen cabinets
- Stain the front door and replace the doorknob and deadbolt
- Professional painting
- Install smoke detectors and door stops where necessary

Numbers

Initial Costs and Assumptions
- Purchase Price: $35,000
- Settlement Fees: $658 (closing fees, insurance)
- Estimated Repairs: $10,000
- Resale Price: $85,000 owner financed

Actual costs
- Holding costs: $933.45 (interest, taxes, insurance, utilities)
- Closing costs: $273.00

Final Numbers
- Repairs: $5,409.75
- Total closing costs: $273.00
- Actual resale price: $85,000
- Actual profit: $42,725.80

Things are much different with these owner-financed deals. We don't use a Realtor to sell, so it's much easier, but you don't get a big chunk of profit right away. We are now receiving payments from the buyer for the next 30 years.

Before photos: http://www.flippingjunkie.com/2011/perp-house

Front Yard Stink House

This was a 3 bedroom, 2 bath, 1000-square-foot house. This is the one where it smelled so bad, my wife wouldn't come in and could still smell it while she waited in the yard.

This lead came in Week 22 and was under contract by Week 25. After holding it for a little while, we decided to wholesale it since we had a few other rehabs underway at the time. The sale closed in Week 34.

Timeline
- Purchase date: September 21, 2011
- Resale date: November 1, 2011

Numbers
- Purchase price: $19,000
- Settlement fees (buy side): $1,271 (title policy, closing fee, insurance)
- Holding costs: $79.17
- Property taxes: $1,615 (agreed to pay 2011 taxes when I bought)
- Repairs: $2,950
- Resale price: $45,000
- Settlement fees (sell side): $328 (closing fee, document prep)
- Profit: $19,756

Audi House

This was a 4 bedroom, 2.5 bathroom, 2200-square-foot house built in 1968. It is a single-story in a good neighborhood. The house was filled with the previous owner's belongings (a ton of stuff) and we sold it just the way we bought it, with everything still in it.

This lead came in Week 25 and was wholesaled in Week 30.

Timeline
- Purchase date: September 29, 2011
- Resale date: October 28, 2011

The Numbers
- Purchase price: $65,000
- Settlement fees (buy side): $1,296 (title policy, closing fee, insurance, loan fee)
- Resale price: $87,000
- Settlement fees (sell side): $1,693 (closing fee, half of the title policy, taxes, loan interest)
- Profit: $19,011

Not bad for just buying and selling. I'd rather do these all day long than rehab and wait to sell. The ARV for this house is about $160,000 and I estimated the repairs at about $25k.

Rambo House

This was a deal from later on in the process. The family wanted to make money on the house, but my MAO was too low to allow it. We agreed I'd pay exactly what they owe and close quickly. The first mention of this deal is in Week 31.

Timeline
- Purchase date: September 21, 2011
- Resale date: November 1, 2011

The Numbers
- Purchase price: $19,000
- Settlement fees: $1,661.37
- Holding and Repair Costs: $5,587.32
- Resale price: $45,000
- Profit: $17,751.31

Just like with the Audi House, this is a great profit for just buying and selling.

The Bottom Line

In total, over 34 weeks, we bought 11 houses, 6 of which were rehabbed and resold, 4 were wholesaled, and 1 we rehabbed and kept for ourselves. We got a total of 505 leads from all the marketing we did, and netted nearly $250,000 in total, not including bird-dog fees.

As you can see, the process does have its ups and downs. There are several times where frustrations can make you feel like quitting, but if you can keep your cool, treat everyone you encounter with respect, and just keep going, the rewards are worth it. Not only do you make a nice living, but you can take time off when you want to, take on as much work as you choose, and have time left over to spend with your family. In the end, it's more than worth it.

Final Note

Thank You

Thank you for reading this book. May your path to financial freedom be even more exciting.

Where to Go from Here

Be sure to visit FlippingJunkie.com for new adventures and the best tips on flipping houses you will find anywhere. Make sure you subscribe as I share all the best stuff by email. If you don't, may your dreams be haunted by the Halloweenists. ;)

Have time for more house flipping goodness in your car or when you're running? Check out the Flipping Junkie Podcast on iTunes. I'd love for you to subscribe and get to know me better. I interview other successful house flippers and share new insights as we gain them in our business. Check out the podcast!

My one best piece of advice is, if you're ready to get started, focus your energy on getting leads. Nothing else matters if you don't have leads. If you're not sure where to start, set up a real estate investor website — that's how I get the majority of my leads and deals. Lucky for you, I can help you out. Just visit http://leadpropeller.com/flippinghousesexposed and find out how you can have your real estate investor website up and running within as little as 15 minutes.

Managing leads, setting up automatic follow-up reminders, mailing written offers with the click of a button, analyzing deals, determining repair costs, keeping track of cost per lead and cost per deal, managing direct mail campaigns among other things if what flipping houses is all about. You can make your life *so much* easier with my lead management software. Have access to all of your data from your mobile devices so that you can run your house flipping business like a real business, no matter where you are. Visit http://flippilot.com to find out more about this incredible software.

Also...if you really enjoyed this adventure, please take a moment right now to leave a review on Amazon.com. (I've got to show my family it was worth the time putting all of this together.)

Thank you!

Danny Johnson

About the Author

Danny Johnson has been flipping houses since 2003. He left his job as a software developer to be a full-time real estate investor in 2005.

Danny and his wife, Melissa, have flipped around 500 houses and absolutely love the business and what it's done for their family and their lives. They have 5 kids and live in San Antonio, TX. Recently, Danny and Melissa started the company FreedomDriven LLC to help busy real estate investors achieve true freedom through training, software, and lead generation services.

Since 2010, Danny has been blogging about flipping houses at FlippingJunkie.com. He's more recently started a podcast where he interviews other real estate investors from across the country. The podcast, The Flipping Junkie Podcast, is a series that covers everything from mindset to marketing to building a team, estimating repairs, finding the money for deals, rehabbing, and wholesaling. Be sure to check it out for in-depth information on how to flip houses.

Danny, still having a passion for software development, has created several software products for real estate investors. LeadPropeller provides real estate investor website systems for house flippers to generate motivated seller leads. His websites are generating tens of thousands of leads for thousands of investors all over the world.

Danny and Melissa have recently created a Facebook group where they love interacting with other investors. The group is called 'Flip Pilot.' Search for the group on Facebook and request an invite. They share ideas on how to work more *on* your flipping business than *in* it.

You may have noticed an aviation theme with FreedomDriven, LeadPropeller, and FlipPilot — that's because Danny is a private pilot and loves to fly his Van's RV6 in his spare time.

Made in the USA
Coppell, TX
09 March 2020

16660405R00138